Writing on Shakespeare

Writing on Shakespeare's Walls

THE HISTORIC GRAFFITI IN THE GUILD CHAPEL,
STRATFORD-UPON-AVON

Pamela Devine

YouCaxton Publications
Oxford & Shrewsbury

Copyright © Pamela Devine 2020

The Author asserts the moral right to
be identified as the author of this work.

ISBN 978-1-913425-20-3
Published by YouCaxton Publications 2020
YCBN: 01

All rights reserved. No part of this publication may be reproduced, stored in a retrieval system, or transmitted in any form or by any means, electronic, mechanical, photocopying, recording or otherwise, without the prior permission of the author.

This book is sold subject to the condition that it shall not, by way of trade or otherwise, be lent, resold, hired out or otherwise circulated without the author's prior consent in any form of binding or cover other than that in which it is published and without a similar condition including this condition being imposed on the subsequent purchaser.

YouCaxton Publications
enquiries@youcaxton.co.uk

Contents

Introduction vii

1. The Guild Chapel today 1
2. Masons' marks and more 6
3. Medieval graffiti 15
4. After the Reformation 61
5. 1616 onwards 75
6. Beyond the seventeenth century 83

Bibliography 95

Index 103

Introduction

For many people, the word 'graffiti' has negative undertones and conjures up images of spray-painted walls in inner cities. Graffiti was not always considered undesirable and anti-social: writing on walls was once not only recognised and tolerated, it was commonplace and even encouraged, carved using whatever sharp implement was to hand.

In the last few years, there has been a great deal of interest in the historic graffiti carved onto church walls and what it can tell us about the thoughts and beliefs of those who left it. In the past, it has been largely overlooked and undervalued as a historical source with little attempt made to record the thousands of symbols, pictures and textual inscriptions that cover our religious buildings. Now, new discoveries and interpretations are emerging almost daily, broadening our knowledge and adding to a growing body of material. The graffiti in the Chapel of the Guild of the Holy Cross in Stratford-upon-Avon is particularly important because of the building's association with William Shakespeare and his family. They would have been very familiar with the Chapel - it was a central and permanent feature in their lives. The Chapel's graffiti is also important because it is unique within Stratford: there is no other building in the town with such a broad range of historic graffiti. In the properties connected with Shakespeare, only a few isolated examples of graffiti survive even though writing on walls was very much a part of his world. The Chapel's graffiti gives us a glimpse into that world.

Graffiti was often, although not always, the work of more ordinary people who could not afford to leave their mark in the way wealthy patrons did. Most surviving evidence - manuscripts, artwork, the fabric and furnishings of churches themselves - tells us what the Church wanted people to believe and how they wanted them to behave, but what did people really think? Although much is still speculative and sometimes we can only guess at the intentions behind what could be intricate and time-consuming inscriptions, graffiti brings to life the ordinary, the illiterate and the everyday, so often excluded from historical accounts. It shows us what concerned people, how they felt about themselves and the innate need to be remembered.

Stratford-upon-Avon is fortunate in being the town where William Shakespeare was born as many of the town's records have been saved as a result. The *Register of the Guild of the Holy Cross* has also survived and it provides a detailed list of the members of the Guild between 1406 and 1534, revealing the names, occupations, social status, and fines (entry fees) they paid for membership. While it gives a wonderful insight into the people who were members of the Guild, it cannot reveal the ways in which they interacted with the Guild buildings or how they 'lived' their faith in the way that graffiti does. The graffiti that has been left in the Guild Chapel sheds light on the actual thoughts and beliefs of the people who have used the space, and tells the story of the Chapel and its famous neighbour from an entirely new perspective. It provides an invaluable insight into normally intangible and elusive elements in the building's history, putting flesh on the bones of the building in a way that has never been possible before.

At first glance, there appears to be little more than a few random scratches on the walls of the Chapel, but the more you look, the more you see. Since 2016, I have been working to identify, document and interpret the building's historic graffiti and over two hundred marks have been recorded so far, only a small proportion of which are modern. Some of the graffiti has been inscribed onto areas hard to photograph; the curved surfaces of narrow pillars make lighting and photography particularly challenging. The survival of so much historic graffiti is testament to the fact that graffiti was once viewed very differently - there has been no attempt to erase it. The lack of attention the Chapel has sometimes suffered, living as it does in the shadow of Stratford-upon-Avon's parish church, Holy Trinity (where Shakespeare is buried), may have helped preserve it. Ironically, the faintness of the Chapel's graffiti, now mostly invisible without a torch, may also have prolonged its survival, but how much longer will it last and how much has already been lost?

Centuries of wear and tear may have taken their toll, but the graffiti that has survived in the Guild Chapel is typical of the sort of historic graffiti commonly found across the country, the nature of it perhaps reflecting Stratford's position as the quintessential rural town, at all times trying to steer a middle course. To fully understand the graffiti, we must first understand the Chapel so chapters one and two give a short overview of the Chapel today and a brief history of the Guild.

This provides some context for the rest of the book which focuses on the graffiti itself and what it can tell us.

Some marks embody Church orthodoxy while others seem to draw on folklore and superstition. Others still are commemorative and territorial in nature. The graffiti the members of the Guild left shows us what concerned people on the eve of William Shakespeare's birth. Medieval graffiti had meaning and function and the inscriptions people carved were like private prayers immortalised in stone. Shakespeare would have accepted it as a normal part of daily life, he may even have carved some of his own. Later graffiti in the Chapel provides a snapshot of how beliefs and superstitions evolved during Shakespeare's lifetime as Protestantism replaced Catholicism in England after the Reformation. In the early-modern period, graffiti in churches gradually became more secular and memorial. The limited amount of more modern graffiti in the Chapel, even though Stratford was the focus of Shakespearian heritage and literary pilgrimage, tells its own story; it reflects the change in attitude towards graffiti in churches after the seventeenth century and more generally as the Victorian period progressed.

Graffiti brings us face to face with the people who have come and gone from the Chapel for over five hundred years – the walls really do talk!

1. The Guild Chapel today

The grade one listed Chapel of the Guild of the Holy Cross in Stratford-upon-Avon is one of the best examples in northern Europe of a purpose-built medieval guild chapel. It also exemplifies the strength of mercantile arts patronage in the late-medieval period. Stratford Town Trust is custodian of the building putting it in the unusual position of being a religious building administered by a secular body, a condition that goes back to 1553 when a royal charter established the Corporation of Stratford and the corporation was granted ownership of the Chapel.

Fig. 1. The Guild Chapel of the Holy Cross, Stratford-upon-Avon.

The Chapel stands at the corner of Church Street and Chapel Lane at the heart of Stratford's medieval street plan (figs 1 and 5). Although the exterior was largely refaced in the second half of the twentieth century, it still closely resembles the original fifteenth-century construction, and remains one of Stratford's most impressive buildings. The Chapel itself is a simple two-cell structure consisting of a low chancel and a tall, impressive nave containing four full-height windows now filled with modern clear glass. The chancel windows contain twentieth-century stained glass. The Chapel's ornate north porch is currently the main entrance. Originally, it would have had an open archway but it is now fitted with a seventeenth-century door. The fifteenth-century door in the south wall of the nave survives and leads to the adjoining Guild buildings (fig. 2). At the western end of the building there is a large square tower which, today, is accessed from inside the Chapel.

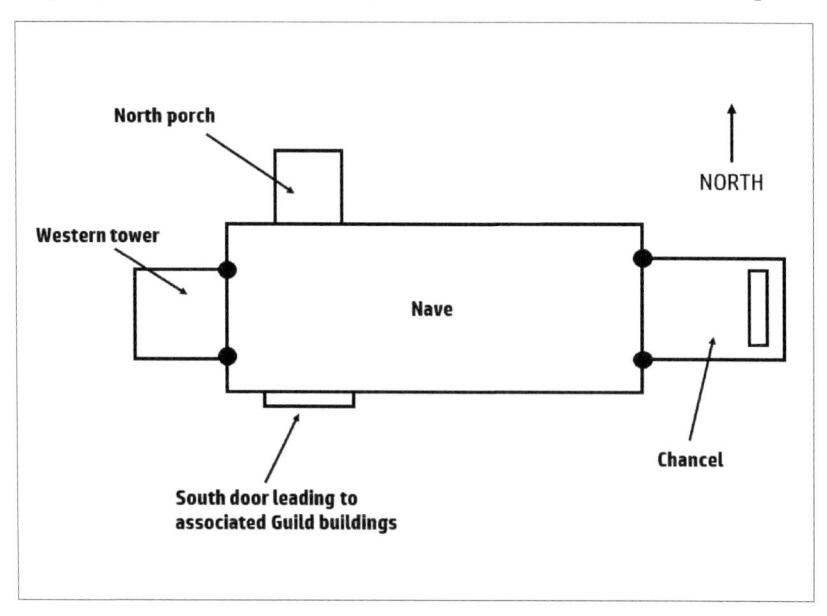

Fig. 2. Plan of the Chapel showing key structural features.

Within the Chapel, the tower originally opened onto the nave through a tall and elegant arch. The west door and window would have been visible from inside, creating a balancing visual interest with the window at the east end. The west door is no longer used and the tower arch is now filled by the organ pipes and a door leading to a panelled vestry and the tower steps beyond. The present organ was installed in 2014, funded by Stratford Town Trust and the Friends of the Guild Chapel. It was inaugurated by HRH Prince Charles (fig. 3).

The internal walls of the Chapel were once covered with a striking and elaborate medieval painting scheme, stressing the inevitability of death and judgement, which Guild members would have recognised and understood. It was designed to fit specifically within the Chapel's architectural structure and in relation to its decorative features, the intention being that it would be seen and understood holistically. For a small guild chapel outside of London, the wall-paintings were expensive and sophisticated. They are important today because they form an almost complete pre-Reformation painting scheme which remains *in situ,* where the design was conceived and executed as one piece of work at the same time – there are few comparable examples in northern Europe.

Fig. 3. The west wall and tower arch, now filled with the organ pipes.

Although some of the colours have now faded, the *Doom* or *Day of Judgement* painting over the chancel arch still has enormous impact (fig. 4). For medieval Christians it was a powerful reminder of the widespread expectation that Judgement Day was imminent, and burning hell-fires awaited if you failed to lead a good life and have a 'good death'. The omnipresent Jesus would have gazed down from above the three-dimensional rood (crucifix), which rested against the chancel wall and provided a dramatic reminder of Jesus's atoning death on the cross. The silhouettes of the rood and its flanking figures show where they were positioned, and tell us that they were in place before the painting was created.

The *Doom* was cleaned and stabilised in 2016 together with the poem on the lower west wall, *Erthe upon Erthe*, an allegory on death written in middle English (fig. 58)[1]. The poem talks explicitly about

---

1 The poem *Erthe upon Erthe* was covered by wooden panelling until October 2016 when the panelling was permanently removed for the painting to be cleaned and stabilised.

the horrors of purgatory, while on the other side of the west wall, a painting, still hidden at the time of writing, depicted either an allegorical female figure representing Pride, or *The Whore of Babylon*.[2] The blatant message in the now fragmentary *Dance of Death* along the north wall of the nave is that death comes to everyone and is the ultimate equaliser: God, in his final judgement, is no respecter of rank or position. The *Lyf of Adam* on the opposite wall has survived better and forms a preface to the *Legend of the Holy Cross* paintings once in the chancel, an obvious choice for a guild which placed such importance on the Holy Cross and its associated legends. On the upper west wall, faint images of brave St George and the martyr Thomas Becket remain, role models of good, 'manly' Christian virtue that members of the Guild could aspire to. Saints, painted in the niches between the windows in the nave, were familiar and sympathetic mediators between God and the Guild members gathered below.

Fig. 4. The nave, facing east into the chancel.

---

2 Purgatory was the place medieval Christians believed they had to go after death to atone for their sins before progressing to heaven.

By the end of the eighteenth century, the Chapel was in a poor state. It was extensively renovated in 1804-05 when the rotting fifteenth-century timber roof was replaced and the present plaster ceiling installed. Despite the new, lower ceiling, the nave of the Chapel remains tall and imposing (fig. 4). The tiles laid in the nave in the early-1800s have survived. Wall-panelling fitted not long afterwards was removed in the mid-twentieth century under the direction of the Westminster architect, Stephen Dykes Bower, together with the old organ and a wooden gallery that had been installed at the west end of the nave. Dykes Bower designed the present timber panelling and pews, now of historic interest in their own right. The panelling remains on the north and south walls of the nave, and the west wall of the nave on the north side. Some of the panels can be opened. In the chancel, the panelling reaches dado rail height, the walls above being rendered and painted.

2. Masons' marks and more

A BRIEF HISTORY OF THE GUILD

William Shakespeare (1564-1616) would have been very familiar with the Guild Chapel. It is situated between the grammar school he almost certainly attended as a boy and the site of the house known as New Place that once occupied the plot on the corner of Chapel Street and Chapel Lane (fig. 5). Shakespeare bought New Place for his family in 1597. It is thought he wrote most of his post-1597 plays here and it is assumed that this is where he died. The Chapel Shakespeare knew had been largely rebuilt in the late-1490s, but there have been Guild buildings on this site since at least the mid-thirteenth century. Even at that early date, Stratford-upon-Avon was a thriving market town, and Church Street and Chapel Street important conduits linking the 'Old Town' around the parish church of Holy Trinity and the new town to the north.

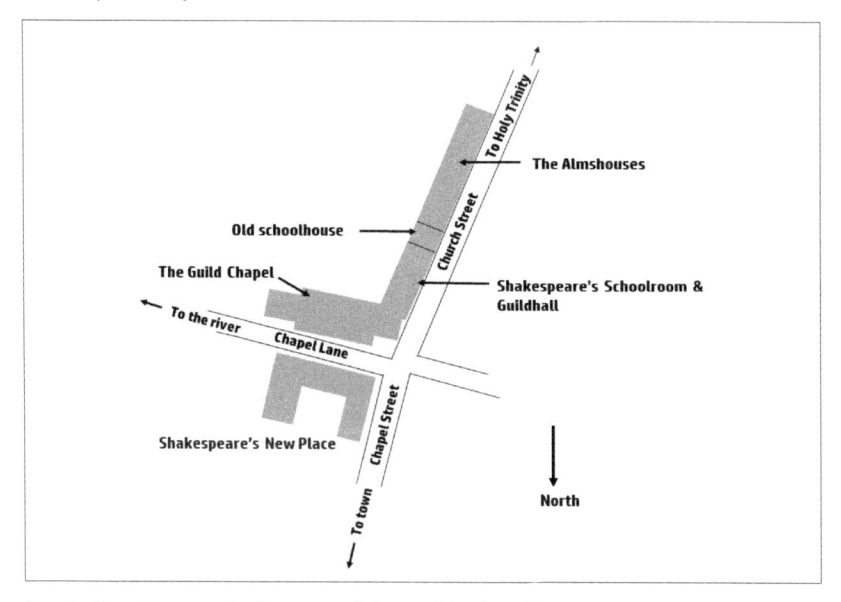

Fig. 5. Plan showing the location of the Guild Chapel between New Place and Shakespeare's Schoolroom.

The actual date the Guild of the Holy Cross was founded in Stratford-upon-Avon is not known, but it was probably in the late-twelfth, or early-thirteenth, century. It was a religious and charitable guild offering members security in times of need, and prayers for the salvation of their souls after death to speed their passage through purgatory. As well as offering religious benefits, membership of the Guild provided social opportunities, schooling for members' sons and the chance to participate in an extensive business network. Membership was open to everyone as long as they could afford the fine, and between 1406 and 1534 the names of approximately 8000 members are recorded in the *Register of the Guild of the Holy Cross*. They ranged from merchants, skilled craftsmen, yeomen and their wives to knights, esquires and gentlemen. There were a few nobles and a number of clergymen although the Guild was firmly under the control of the laity. There was even a royal connection. The Guild accounts for 1478-79 record an entry fine for Prince Edward, the son of Edward IV, who later disappeared, along with his brother, after being imprisoned in the Tower of London on the orders of Richard III. Admitted to the Guild at the same time was the powerful Sir Anthony Rivers, the prince's guardian and governor, and brother of Elizabeth Woodville, Edward IV's queen. Sir Anthony was beheaded in 1483, also on the orders of Richard III. One wonders where the loyalties of Guild members lay and whether prayers were ever said for the prince and his uncle?

At first, an altar was maintained by the Guild in the north aisle of Holy Trinity Church where a college of chaplains employed by the Guild said mass for the souls of deceased members and their ancestors. The Guild also sold indulgences and when members died, it arranged a solemn procession, a requiem mass and a burial feast.[3] It has been said that membership of the Guild was a little like having an insurance policy for getting into heaven.

The building which forms the present Guild Chapel is thought to date from around 1269-70. This is when the Bishop of Worcester issued a charter granting the Guild permission to set up a hospital, or place of hospitality, to support a resident community of needy priests from the diocese, and nine poor, sick or aged Stratfordians. The hospital was to consist of a refectory, dormitory and infirmary, to be manned by a resident warden and chaplain. The charter also

---

[3] Indulgences were 'good works' or charitable acts that had to be performed to reduce the punishment you might have to endure in purgatory for sins you had committed, before you progressed to heaven. The complicated system was open to abuse and it increasingly became possible to 'buy' indulgences from the Church. The Reformation in the sixteenth century brought the practice of buying indulgences to an end.

reveals that an oratory or chapel was to be built for the private use of the residents and those serving the hospital. It was usual for medieval infirmaries to have a private oratory, with an open screen supporting a carved and decorated cross dividing the two chambers. The exact layout of the Guild buildings is not certain, but documentary evidence suggests the oratory was in what is now the chancel; the lower sections of the south and east walls of the chancel are still constructed from the thirteenth-century rubblework. The hospital was probably in what is now the nave. It would have been a half-timbered structure with wattle and daub in-fill panels and the roofline would probably have aligned with that of the chancel which would have been more steeply pitched than now. The foundation charter refers to needy brethren *and sisters* suggesting there were additional residential quarters for women. Their chambers would have been separated from those of the clerics and lay brethren, and were most likely situated where the current Guildhall is. Despite the facilities it offered, the hospital only functioned for about twenty years after which the building was leased. The Guild continued to confine its religious and social activities to the parish church. Records show that by 1403, the former infirmary hall was being used by the Guild again, this time as a meeting hall and for its four annual feasts.

The Guild of the Holy Cross became extremely powerful within Stratford and functioned like an early local government. Indeed, religious guilds across the country underpinned the development of medieval towns and the rise of civic leadership. As the membership of the guild in Stratford grew, it accumulated considerable wealth and property, and when the old infirmary became too small as a meeting house, the Guild built the adjoining Guildhall and, a few years later, a new schoolhouse (fig. 5). This was a major rebuilding programme, reflecting the prosperity of the Guild. Archaeological surveys and dendrochronology, or tree ring dating, have shown that the Guildhall dates from 1417-18 while the school dates from 1427. Although the dates are less specific for the almshouses still visible in Church Street, they have been dendro-dated to the early-1500s. They are still used as almshouses today.

With the growth of the Guild, members wanted their own chapel and, now that they had the new Guildhall, the old hospital was converted into a place of worship for the Guild members and consecrated. The Guild was now independent of the parish church.

2. Masons' marks and more

The stone nave, porch and tower we see today were added in the mid- to late-1490s, with the chancel being extended slightly to meet the new structure. Most construction work utilised the materials most readily available locally as they were cheaper and more convenient. In medieval Stratford, timber from the densely wooded area to the north of the town was the preferred building material; stone was used sparingly and only on the most important buildings. The Guild Chapel was one of only a handful of buildings in Stratford to be built in stone.

Part of being a good Christian entailed doing 'good works' in order to get into heaven more quickly, and it is thanks to the local merchant, Hugh Clopton (c.1440-1496), one-time Master of the Guild and former Lord Mayor of London, that the Chapel's nave, tower and porch were built in stone and the walls painted. Hugh Clopton was one of the wealthiest merchants in London and the original owner of New Place, which he built for himself in 1483. The considerable sum of money Clopton intended spending on rebuilding the Chapel is indicative of the strength of medieval lay piety, which peaked between the fourteenth and sixteenth centuries. Clopton was promoting a very particular set of religious beliefs and practices and, intentionally or not, he was also making a powerful statement about his own status and identity.[4]

Clopton's 1496 will stipulated that the work on the Chapel be completed according to the plans he had drawn up with Thomas *'Dowland, and diverse other masons for the beldyng and setting up of the Chapell'* and *'that the saide masons sufficiently and ably doo and fynysshe the same with good and true werkmanshipp'*. The marks of the masons who worked on the Chapel are still visible on the walls over 500 years after they were created (fig. 6). These marks are essentially the 'signatures' of the masons who worked on the building. There was no single system of marking stonework, but generally masons marked the stones so their output could be monitored by the paymaster. There were two types of mark: assembly marks and banker marks. The ones in the Chapel are banker marks, used by the masons to identify their own work.

It seems the decision to use marks or not lay with someone other than the masons themselves because when masons were paid regular

---

[4] Hugh Clopton is often, mistakenly, given the title 'Sir'; he was never knighted and, in his will, he describes himself as 'citizen, mercer and alderman'.

wages, the masonry was not marked. Masons' marks are found on stone buildings where the stone is finished to a high degree, as it was in the Chapel. They can be seen in most areas of a church and, unlike graffiti, are often located high up on arches or other out-of-the-way places, in areas that can only be reached with scaffolding or a ladder. They tend to stand out from graffiti owing to their repetition in close proximity. Often it is only by looking at the tools that might have been used, for example, a chisel or punch, and the context of a mark, that it is possible to distinguish between masons' marks and graffiti.

Fig. 6. Mason's mark, south wall, right of the south door.

Masons' marks are typically neat and well cut since they were made by people skilled in using sharp tools. Masons did not spend time cutting elaborate marks, most consisted of a series of between four to six straight lines - curves were rarely used (figs 7 and 8). Being relatively simple, they could be quickly and easily reproduced. Some were based on letter-types, and it may be that these referred to masons' names although, as few masons were literate, they would have had to learn how to cut them.

Records of the masons who worked on the great churches and cathedrals of medieval Europe sometimes survive giving us names, rates of pay, types of work done and so on. For smaller churches, it is rare for masons to be individually named in accounts, and records seldom survive. While the names of the individual masons in the Chapel might be long forgotten, Clopton's will does give us Dowland's name.

2. Masons' marks and more

Fig. 7. Mason's mark repeated throughout the Chapel.

Fig. 8. Mason's mark, north door surround.

Dowland was most likely the Master Mason in charge of the 1490s rebuild and, as such, would have been responsible for the Chapel's design, overseeing the project and organising the other masons. It was a respected and well-paid occupation, and a top mason could expect to earn a substantial income.

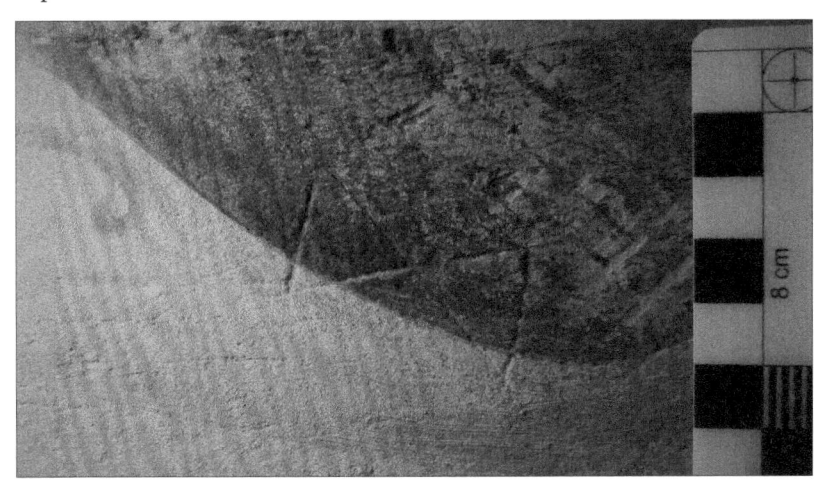

Fig. 9. Mason's mark, west wall, also found on the chancel arch.

As masons' marks were generally allocated on a job-by-job basis, identifying individual masons is problematic. It is sometimes possible to do so, but marks were mostly site-specific and re-used: few masons used the same mark throughout their working lives. What masons' marks can do is show phases of construction, give an idea of the number of masons employed on a particular site and so on. Underneath the *Day of Judgement* painting over the chancel arch, one mark appears repeatedly (fig. 9). It seems the mason with this mark was responsible for preparing the bulk of the blocks for this area;

his mark also appears on the west wall. Judging from the number of different masons' marks found in the Chapel so far, it would appear Dowland's team consisted of at least half a dozen masons.

Medieval masons had many skills and, in addition to squaring blocks, undertook sculptural work and the cutting of inscriptions; there was no distinction drawn between masons and sculptors as there is now. Masons have been known to carve their own faces in the work they created. Some of the carved faces flanking the niches between the windows in the nave of the Guild Chapel have survived (figs 10 and 11). Perhaps these are the faces of the Chapel's masons?

Figs 10 & 11. Faces in the stonework of the Guild Chapel.

Hugh Clopton, it seems, was determined to secure his place in heaven. In his will, he not only directed that the Guild Chapel be completed, he bequeathed £50 towards the building of a cross aisle in Holy Trinity Church and bestowed money on a variety of good causes. He also instructed that, should he die in Stratford, he was to be buried in an elaborate tomb constructed in a very privileged position in the north aisle of Holy Trinity, where a college of priests would pray for his soul.[5] Clopton's motives in rebuilding the Guild Chapel may have been entirely altruistic, but arguably he was buying his place in heaven. Wealthy elites would compete to build the biggest and best private church, believing God would reward them with a passport to heaven. Perhaps Clopton intended the new chapel next door to his house to be, in effect, his personal chantry chapel. Paying for it to be rebuilt and painted was certainly a way of ensuring he was remembered in perpetuity. An image made in the early-1800s of

---

5 Hugh Clopton was actually buried in the chapel of St Katherine in the parish church of St Margaret Lothbury, London, as directed in his will should he die in London or within 20 miles of the city. The medieval church perished in the Great Fire of London in 1666; the current church was rebuilt by Sir Christopher Wren. It is not known what happened to Hugh Clopton's remains.

a wall-painting once above the priest's door in the Chapel's chancel, shows a large figure amongst other, smaller figures, all gazing at a crucifix. It has been suggested that the larger figure might be Hugh Clopton. It was not unusual for notable patrons to be represented within a church, exhorting the devout to pray for them. If it was Clopton's image in what was, at the time, very much a separated space, it emphasises his status and demonstrates the complex relationship that exists between religious art and its benefactors. Despite the clear message in the Chapel's wall-paintings that death was the ultimate equaliser, it must have seemed to more ordinary Guild members that their social and economic superiors could aspire to a higher spiritual plane.

It is a shame Clopton died before he could see his plans completed.

3. Medieval graffiti

BELIEFS AND SUPERSTITIONS ON THE EVE OF SHAKESPEARE'S BIRTH

There is an enduring fascination with medieval religious art which the recent interest in medieval graffiti taps into, as we try to understand something that appears to modern eyes to be otherworldly. The medieval Church formed a community in which everyone was immersed from birth to death. The formal observation of religion impacted on almost every aspect of life; it gave structure to people's earthly lives and offered salvation in death. Churches were a place of mystery, halfway between heaven and earth, and the rites performed therein had a mystical air. The beliefs and practices dictated by the Church can be seen in the fabric and furnishings that remain in our medieval churches, but they only tell a partial story. They cannot tell us what people actually thought or how they lived out their beliefs in practice: 'folk' beliefs existed alongside orthodox religion in an effort to provide an extra layer of spiritual protection.

People believed their lives were directed by mysterious forces. Some forces were good, like angels and the heavens, while others were harmful and made you vulnerable to demons and malign spirits. Magic was widely recognised as something that could change your life, for better and for worse. It provided solutions to a range of problems from the everyday to the extraordinary, problems that could not be resolved in any other way. Witches could be good or bad but all had colluded with the devil in order to work wonders. Good (white) witches, or cunning folk, could heal the sick or find lost and stolen property. Bad (black) witches could cause death and injury, or a bad harvest. The universe itself was an animate body whose every element had a sympathetic relationship to the rest - even colours, letters and numbers possessed magical qualities. It is understandable that people sought to control their lives with objects, rituals and charms designed to attract benevolent spirits and mitigate the evil spirits that were seen everywhere and in everything. Even today we still believe in lucky objects or have little rituals to ease our anxieties, our emotional needs triumphing over rational thought.

3. Medieval graffiti

Inanimate objects were invested with the power to protect and ward off evil. Holy water was considered a particularly powerful agent. Candles blessed at Candlemas were taken home to prolong the protection found in church. Carving graffiti onto church walls was just one more layer of protection in the fight against the forces of evil and, in appropriating the walls of churches, the symbols and markings people drew acquired a symbolic dimension and added spiritual effectiveness. Magic and ritual were central to the medieval Church and the Church did nothing to discourage belief in the protective power of graffiti – these markings were ubiquitous across Europe and broadly understood, the hoped-for benefits the same as from orthodox religious practice.

Apotropaic (from the Greek word *apotropaios*, meaning to turn away evil) inscriptions are popularly known as 'witch marks'. This is misleading as witch marks were marks found on witches' bodies and were a physical sign that witches were in league with the devil. A better term is 'ritual protection mark' or 'Holy sign' as the marks carved onto church walls provided protection from evil spirits for the person who created them and for the area or object onto which they were inscribed.

It is not always possible to strictly define what a ritual protection mark is, and the meaning of graffiti can change depending on the circumstances and contexts in which it is drawn. Dating graffiti is also challenging. It was rarely dated before the mid-sixteenth century, dates only becoming common in the early-seventeenth century, possibly because the regnal year had been used previously. Often it is only possible to say graffiti is pre- or post-Reformation and, even then, there are grey areas as beliefs did not change overnight. Certain trends can indicate a likely period and the subject matter of the graffiti can sometimes provide clues. Broadly speaking, medieval and early-modern graffiti expressed thoughts, beliefs, hopes and fears. The sort of graffiti that gradually started appearing from the mid-sixteenth century onwards - initials, names and dates - is more territorial, a tangible record of a visit or an act of remembrance. The earliest possible date for the graffiti in the Chapel, as it stands today, is the mid- to late-1490s which is when the nave was rebuilt in stone. The bulk of the Chapel's graffiti cannot be closely dated, but much of it is characteristic of the most common inscriptions from the medieval period which is why they have been included in this section.

Hundreds of years of wear and tear means graffiti can sometimes be difficult to see, some marks having been only lightly scratched onto the stonework in the first place. Much is invisible to the naked eye and can only be seen with a torch, ideally tilted to provide a raking light. The Chapel's interior is soft limestone, scrubbed and repainted many times and heavily abraded in places, so it is likely a great deal will have been destroyed or obscured. At the time it was carved, however, the graffiti would have been clearly visible, a recognised and tolerated part of religious life, obvious to both the chaplains employed by the Guild and the Guild members. In the Middle Ages, churches were vibrant, colourful places, almost garish to modern eyes, and any graffiti carved onto their decorated surfaces would have stood out plainly. The fact that this graffiti has not been defaced or destroyed is indicative of how tolerated it was.

Medieval graffiti distribution in churches and cathedrals appears to be random, but patterns do exist, and the Guild Chapel seems to be typical of the general rule. Ritual protection marks are common around doorways, particularly the main south door, windows, archways and in porches, anywhere through which, it was thought, evil spirits could enter a building. These portals were considered vulnerable as they could not be permanently closed off. Ritual protection marks appear to be an attempt to maintain these thresholds and prevent malicious forces from outside coming inside. The south west corner of the Chapel has a range of apotropaic markings. The main south door leads directly to the Guildhall and other Guild buildings so Guild members may have accessed the Chapel through this door, perhaps explaining the concentration of ritual protection marks in this area (fig. 12).

Fig 12. South door, nave, Guild Chapel.

In this study, I have focused on the Chapel's nave, the chancel having been re-plastered several times, destroying the *Legend of the Holy Cross* paintings once there as well as any graffiti. In any case, medieval graffiti is typically (although not always) found in the nave rather than the chancel, the latter being reserved for the priests and notable patrons of the church, particularly in pre-Reformation days when the magic of the mass was said behind the rood screen, a wooden screen separating the chancel and nave. The screen created a distinct division between the two spaces ensuring an air of mystery was maintained.

Graffiti is often found in bell towers and the Chapel's bell-tower has revealed small amounts of predominantly twentieth-century graffiti, left by the various tradesmen who have worked in the Chapel, although there are hints of earlier ritual protection graffiti.

What follows is a breakdown of the most interesting graffiti I have found in the Chapel so far.

The VV or conjoined-V symbol

One of the most common ritual protection marks by far is the VV or conjoined-V symbol (fig. 13). The Chapel has several examples, mostly around the south door and on the chancel arch. There are also VV marks on the window frames in the adjoining Guildhall.

Fig. 13. Conjoined-V, chancel arch. H. 3cm. *Image: Terry Galvin.*

In medieval contexts, the symbol is widely recognised as having a close association with the cult of the Virgin Mary, and is said to come from the Latin *Virgo Virginum*, meaning Virgin of Virgins. If so, it may have been an expression of religious devotion, or a call for the intervention or blessing of the Virgin Mary. It might also have been a kind of votive offering to give thanks for prayers answered. The symbol is seen across Europe. It has been suggested that the ritual origins of the symbol lie in Scandinavia, where the sign appeared in runic writing systems. In many areas of the eastern Baltic it is still considered a holy sign associated with life, death and fertility. Whatever the origins of the VV symbol, it does appear to have developed an association with the Virgin Mary as it is sometimes seen in traditional church art, one of the few ritual protection marks that is. Did graffiti copy church art or did church art copy graffiti?

There are five examples in the Chapel of what look like a conjoined-V coupled with the letter I, four by the south door and one on the chancel arch (fig. 14). They may simply be initials, but there is a high incidence of such inscriptions in apotropaic contexts elsewhere so the intention may have been similar. Again, the conjoined-V is sometimes seen alongside the letter I in church art.

Fig. 14. An IW inscription, chancel arch. *Image: Rodger Palmer.*

Some people believe these 'initials' might be a conjoined-V and a Christogram or monogram for Jesus. Christians have long invoked his name, believing in its inherent power.[6] Perhaps combining the conjoined-V with a Christ monogram was perceived as doubling its power. Without in-depth research into the frequency of IW

---
6   The letter I is the first letter of the Greek word for Jesus; it was not until the seventeenth century that the letters I and J were systematically differentiated in the Latin alphabet.

inscriptions and all the other letters and initials carved onto our church walls, cross-referenced with historic naming trends, any interpretation of IW remains speculative. Some work has been done to create meaningful data-sets, but more is needed.

After the Reformation, it seems the association of the conjoined-V with the Virgin Mary gradually faded and the symbol came to have a more secular, folkloric protective function, invested with the power to ward off evil, illness and misfortune, later coming to have more of an association with good luck. The division between ritual protection and good luck is indistinct, but the signs were still being used well into the eighteenth century and have been seen in nineteenth-century contexts. Few other ritual protection marks survive the Reformation.

The VV symbol is often found inverted to look like a capital M, and there is a good example on the east wall of the Chapel's nave (fig. 15). There are also a number of M symbols on the chancel arch. Graffiti M's are sometimes seen turned on their side (fig. 16). In the medieval period, M symbols seem to have had a close association with the Virgin Mary and echo well-known Marian monograms found in church interiors: the crowned M, MR, the M capped by stars and so on.

Fig. 15. An M symbol, east wall of nave. *Image: Terry Galvin.*

Some marks seem to have a life of their own, the meaning changing over time. The origins of M inscriptions are unclear, but, if there was a Marian connection, it is not surprising a number have been found in the Chapel and the Guildhall as the Guild of the Holy Cross was formally associated with the smaller Guild of the Blessed Virgin Mary (and that of St John the Baptist) in 1429. The cult of Marian worship was strongest from the late-1400s to the mid-1500s, exactly the period when members of the Stratford guild might have been carving graffiti onto the Chapel walls.

Fig. 16. An M inscription on the medieval plaster of Stratford's Guildhall.

After the Reformation, many images in churches, particularly those of the Virgin Mary, were destroyed or obliterated, yet the ciphers and monograms relating to Mary were left untouched, even those within the reach of enthusiastic puritans in the seventeenth century. The letter M, as a representation of Mary's name, can still be seen on pre-Reformation church furniture, particularly in the West Country. They were obviously not considered troublesome in the same way that iconic images were, possibly because they had already started to lose their direct association with Marian worship, and graffiti M's had simply become symbols designed to ward-off evil.

Both VV and M symbols are frequently seen on iron firebacks from the fifteenth century right through to the eighteenth century, usually either on their own, prominently in a central position or alongside other protection symbols. The chimney was considered the entry point most at risk from witches or their familiars as it was impossible to close off to evil spirits. Iron itself was thought to have apotropaic properties and was used to ward off witches into the early-twentieth century. Adding ritual protection marks to an iron fireback increased that protection. Iron horseshoes have been found hidden inside fireplaces, along with ritual protection marks such as the VV symbol, so they did not have to be visible to be considered effective. Horseshoes were hung open-end down to trap evil spirits. Today, hanging them open-end down symbolises bad luck – we keep them open side up to bring good fortune. Although they are relatively rare, there are instances of graffiti horseshoes on the walls of both religious and vernacular buildings and they invariably have their open sides facing down.

Crosses

Not surprisingly, the cross, one of Christianity's most important symbols, is also one of the most common forms of apotropaic graffiti. Like other ritual protection marks, crosses are often found in significant numbers in church porches and around doorways, especially the south door. They can be plain and lightly scratched or deeply etched, complicated designs.

Mid-twentieth century refurbishments of the Guild Chapel included the refacing of the exterior of the north porch. The original stone remains on the interior but it is badly worn in places. At some point, a screen was added to divide the porch, creating an inner lobby. The screen was removed during the 1950s renovations. Despite the deterioration of the stone in the Chapel's porch, it is still possible to see crosses that were carved there (fig. 17).

Church porches had greater importance in medieval times and could be highly decorated, reflecting their importance as a gateway to the Christian life. Ritual protection marks would have provided a protective barrier against the harmful influences outside. Although they had no doctrinal role, porches were consecrated spaces and important to the community. A number of services were held there including the marriage ceremony, the churching of new mothers (the blessing given to new mothers after childbirth) and burial services. Porches usually contained a holy water stoup for crossing oneself which had

Fig. 17. Cross, door frame, north porch. *Image: Rodger Palmer.*

the effect of renewing baptismal vows as well as warding off evil. The porch was also used for more mundane administrative purposes and was a sort of parish office where oaths were sworn, bargains made and disputes settled. It is possible graffiti crosses represented a desire for divine approval of the verbal oaths and vows made before the church door, or a hoped-for blessing of agreements made therein.

There is currently no stoup in the porch of the Guild Chapel, and it may be that services such as marriage and baptism were performed at Stratford's parish church, Holy Trinity, although there are references to a font being repaired in the Guild accounts in the 1490s. (The Chapel's current font is early-eighteenth century grey marble.) Guild members formed a close network of merchants, traders and artisans, so it is reasonable to assume the Chapel's porch would have been used for making business deals, exchanging contracts, and so on. The Guild Chapel was well-placed within the trading networks of Stratford's four market places, three of which had market crosses. One of them, the White Cross, had stood outside the Guild Chapel at the junction of Church Street and Chapel Street since at least 1275. It was still there in 1608. The Chapel, a central and significant location for Guild members, must have seen its fair share of transactions in its porch, and perhaps the graffiti crosses carved there were intended as a spiritual endorsement of them.

Fig. 18. An X-shaped cross, H. 6cm, south door surround. *Image: Terry Galvin.*

There is a cluster of lightly inscribed X-shaped crosses to the right of the south door in the nave of the Chapel, an area in churches where crosses are often grouped together (fig. 18). There are also X-shaped crosses on the chancel arch. The X represents the Greek letter 'chi', the first letter of the Greek word for Christ (hence Xmas and so on). It is also known as a saltire or Saint Andrew cross as the saint was crucified on an X-shaped cross and it became his major symbol.

Crosses, in particular the X-shaped cross, are found on all sorts of domestic objects from chimney lintels, iron firebacks, door panels and furniture to amulets and charms, added both by the craftsmen who made them and the occupants. According to one Suffolk blacksmith, an X with two adjacent vertical lines was put on latches, and window and door hinges, because the uprights represented the doorposts and the cross barred the way to all things evil.

Compass-drawn designs or compass wheels

Compass-drawn designs or compass wheels are amongst the most common forms of medieval graffiti, and one of the most common ritual protection marks. There are dozens of different types ranging from simple circles to rosettes or multifoils (also known as hexfoils or daisy-wheels), and other even more complicated geometric designs (fig. 19). Like the VV symbol, they are found all over medieval churches.

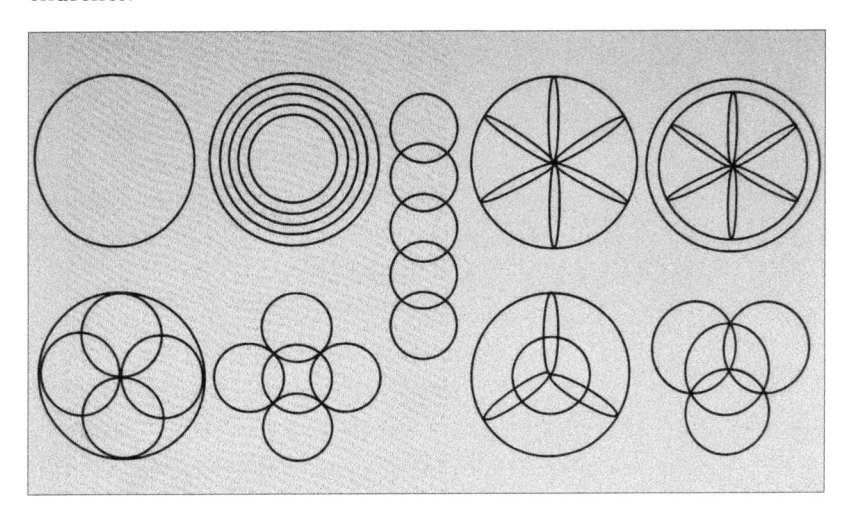

Fig. 19. A small selection of compass-drawn designs.

It was thought compass-wheel graffiti was carved by the masons who built churches as a way of teaching apprentices the basic skills of geometry, or they were made as guides to ensure masons' dividers were properly adjusted. Masons and other artisans often used number theory and geometry in their designs to communicate religious meanings. Occasionally, masons did inscribe working sketches, designs or calculations onto walls, and this graffiti is valuable as manuscript evidence is scarce. Some compass wheels may have been created by medieval masons to calculate the proportions of a building, but current thinking is that most were ritual protection marks designed to bring luck or protect individuals from evil spirits.

Experimental archaeology is testing how they might have been carved but it was most likely some sort of pointed tool like a compass or divider, or even the small domestic knives most people carried around with them. Perhaps women used the scissors or shears often seen hanging from their belts in manuscripts, and it was predominantly women who carved them. Large numbers of compass wheels have been found in and around fonts which have the obvious female association with childbirth and baptism. Women were admitted to the Stratford guild in their own right, not only as wives and daughters, and, even though they were excluded from office-holding and the Guild's decision-making processes, they were able to take part in the rest of the Guild's activities without difficulty.

Exactly when compass wheels were first considered apotropaic is unclear but the symbol itself may have had ancient, pre-Christian origins as the six-petalled rosette or hexfoil has been found on Iron-age objects and appears widely on Roman architectural decorations, military altars, grave markers, and Roman era Jewish artwork. Rosettes are commonly found amongst ancient graffiti at sites such as Pompeii and Herculaneum. They may have been purely decorative or filling motifs, but some research suggests they may have been ancient sun symbols acting as an antidote to darkness. In Romania, they are still used as sun symbols. The appearance of rosettes or hexfoils on objects such as altar stones does suggest a spiritual significance, and it is easy to see why these symbols might have been adopted in early Christianity as the association of the sun with rebirth and renewal coincided with the Christian message, particularly in the rite of baptism. There are several passages in the scriptures which suggest Jesus represents the sun, and Jesus refers to himself as the light of the world, leading people away from darkness, away from evil.

Rosettes may be an alternative to the cross, and derive their power from that association. From the twelfth century onwards, the six-petalled rosette or hexfoil was sometimes used in place of the more traditional equal-armed cross for consecration crosses, and on medieval cross slabs used to mark graves. Consecration crosses were painted onto the walls of a church after it was built. A bishop would consecrate the new building by anointing it with holy oil, typically twelve times inside and twelve times outside. The locations would subsequently be marked by crosses and the crosses painted, normally in red. They were usually carved with compasses or dividers and are sometimes mistaken for ritual protection marks although consecration crosses tend to be much larger.[7] The Guild accounts of 1427-28 reveal that an appropriately named local man, Thomas Payntor, and his son were paid four shillings for eight days' labour *for his colours and for painting and mending the defects in the Guild Chapel*, and two shillings *for making 24 crosses on the walls of the Chapel within and without*. The consecration of the Chapel followed the conversion of the old hospital into a place of worship and the setting up of a second altar to supplement the existing one.

In the Baltic countries, rosettes were known as holy signs and were still being used as part of lay piety until relatively recently. In the West Country, the motif was sometimes known as the symbol or flower of the Passion, reinforcing its association with the cross or crucifix and its power of protection. In France, they are widely known as *rosacea* (rose-like). Images of nature were often used to illustrate medieval Christian teaching and some flowers had a deeply symbolic meaning. The rose symbolises purity and the Virgin Mary, the most beautiful of flowers, and is one of her identifying attributes.[8] In medieval art, the daisy, with its multiple petals, was emblematic of the Christ-child.

The idea that rosettes or multifoils came to have a protective function is strengthened by their use on medieval parish chests (used to store important documents and treasures, and often valuable pieces of furniture in their own right) as well as on beds, pilgrim badges, jewellery and even in books. While it is not known exactly how the different types of compass wheels in medieval churches relate to earlier examples, by the time Guild members were carving graffiti onto the walls of the Guild Chapel, compass-wheel graffiti was commonplace and part of everyday religious practice.

---

7 There are two good examples in Warwick, not far from Stratford, both about a metre in diameter: one in the crypt of the Collegiate Church of St Mary and the other in the Chapel of St James the Great, built over the West Gate. (Unfortunately, the consecration cross in St James's Chapel has recently been covered by information panels secured to the wall.)

8 The rose was also the flower of the Roman goddess of love, Venus, and roses depicted in Roman mosaics can look remarkably like the stylized heraldic form of the rose frequently used to represent the Virgin Mary in medieval art and architecture (not to mention the Lancastrian rose).

The one thing all compass-wheel graffiti have in common is their endless lines. People believed demons and evil spirits were attracted by lines and, once they had been drawn into the never-ending lines of compass wheels, they were trapped or pinned to the wall, forever trying to follow the line to its end and that part of the building was thus protected. This idea can be seen in other apotropaic graffiti, such as the Solomon's Knot (fig. 20). Again, similar ideas can be seen in the pre-Christian period.

Fig. 20. Solomon's Knot graffiti, All Saints Church, Litcham, Norfolk.

Complex labyrinth-like patterns were incorporated into mosaics all across the Roman world and many that survive can be found in Roman bath-houses. These geometric patterns are considered to be apotropaic because they appear alongside other images characterised as such, in some cases in conjunction with patterns analogous to medieval rosettes. Stripped naked for the bathing experience, perhaps Romans felt vulnerable and in need of protection from evil spirits or wanted to subvert the harmful gaze of others.

While the Chapel has no extant rosettes or multifoils, it does have other types of compass-wheel graffiti. They appear to be either single circles or sets of concentric circles. In Christianity, a single circle has symbolic importance as it represents God, or eternity. Medieval scholars drew on classical scholars and saw a connection between science and the divine, particularly in areas such as geometry, astrology and astronomy, and circles were considered inherently

3. Medieval graffiti

divine. The ancient Greeks, from whom the Romans adopted and adapted so much, believed the circle was the perfect shape – it was eternal, without beginning or end, and a perfectly balanced whole. Graffiti circles may have developed out of these ideas and came to be associated with offering protection.

The most obvious compass-wheel in the Guild Chapel is on the door surround in the south wall of the nave (figs 21 and 22). It appears to have consisted of three overlapping circles, perhaps representing the Holy Trinity to give it added potency. In a Christian context, wherever symbols were grouped in threes, the intention seems to have been to enforce the meaning. The number three was highly significant as it represented the equality of God, the Son and the Holy Spirit. The equilateral triangle is one of the oldest Christian symbols for the Holy Trinity, and graffiti triangles are commonly found inscribed onto church walls. Two triangles have been found in the Guild Chapel and they do not appear to be masons' marks. Apotropaic magic often incorporated symbols used three times, sometimes multiplied by three again to make nine, the number nine being the ultimate trinitarianism. Although they are subverting it for diabolical purposes, the three witches in *Macbeth* use the power of nine when they chant, '*Thrice to thine and thrice to mine and thrice again to make up nine*' (Shakespeare, *Macbeth*, act 1, scene 3).

Fig. 21. Remains of a compass wheel. H. 10 cm. South door, nave. *Image: Terry Galvin.*

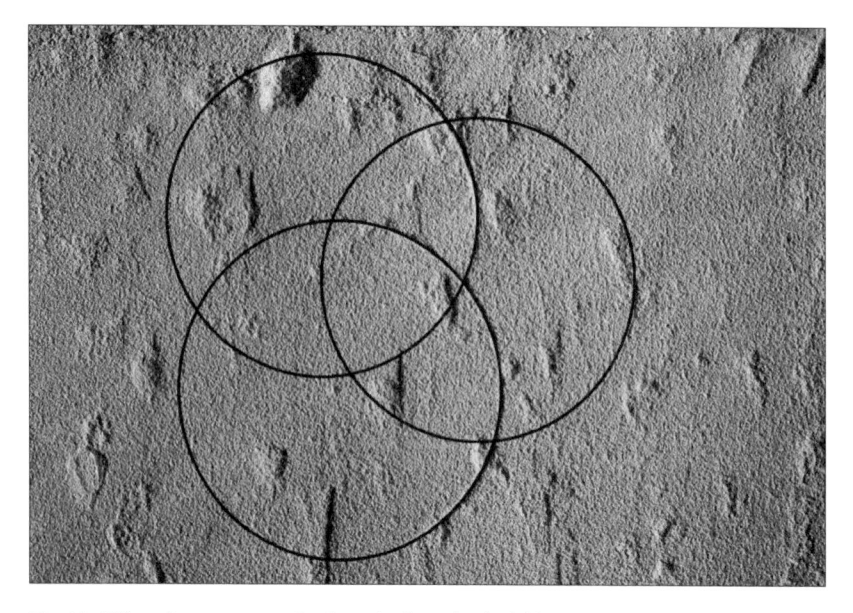

Fig 22. What the compass wheel might have looked like. H. 10 cm. South door, nave. *Image: adapted from an image by Terry Galvin.*

The incompleteness of the compass wheel by the Chapel's south door is most likely the result of wear and tear. However, amongst the mass of medieval graffiti elsewhere, there is evidence that some graffiti, especially compass-wheel graffiti, was deliberately left unfinished. Current thinking is that the intention of whoever carved them may not have been a desire for protection at all. Most medieval curses relied on an inversion of normal practice to invoke the opposite effect and it is possible that these unfinished examples are invoking a curse or a prayer for divine retribution against someone who has sinned against the inscriber. The Church fully accepted ritual protection marks and devotional graffiti, and probably viewed curses in much the same way, especially as the Old Testament seems to promise that God would not ignore appeals from those who had been wronged. The existence on church walls of written curses and charms, together with surviving curses and charms in manuscripts and other contexts, seems to support this theory, the origins of which appear to rest, once again, with the Romans. Inscriptions found incised on medieval church walls are strikingly similar to Roman curse tablets, the most famous being the lead curse tablets recovered from the sacred spring within the temple at the Roman baths in Bath. The tablets were deposited in a characteristically Roman ritual, the custom of dropping them into the spring at Bath merely an adaptation of that ritual to fit the peculiarities of a local setting.

There are remnants of numerous compass wheels in the south west corner of the Guild Chapel, although most have now almost disappeared into the stonework and only barely visible arcs remain. One of the most interesting compass-drawn designs to have survived is a set of concentric circles on the west wall, interesting because it appears to have been carved before the wall was painted with the death poem *Erthe upon Erthe* (figs 23 and 24). Normally it is hard to date graffiti, but, because this graffito is beneath the paint, it can be fairly closely dated to within a few years. Hugh Clopton's will suggests the stone nave was built in the mid- to late-1490s and it is believed the walls were painted shortly after. This compass wheel must, therefore, date from the period between the Chapel walls being built in stone and the walls being painted, so the late-1490s or early-1500s.

It is possible some of the compass-drawn graffiti we see on our church walls developed out of magical practices, and people may have carved them onto the spiritually powerful walls of churches in the belief that it would somehow enhance their power. Magic was very much a part of medieval culture, and medieval scholars studied it in the same way they studied the sciences and other disciplines. Medieval manuscripts contain diagrams of the 'magical figures' which formed a key part of a magician's toolkit. Amongst them are magic circles consisting, in part, of two concentric circles. Their purpose was to ward off sudden death and they were activated by the gaze. Medieval 'seeing' was perceived quite differently and was more like a feeling, giving the viewer the sense that they were touching whatever they were looking at. Vision was thought to be a result of beams of light emanating from the eyes. This light would rebound back from the object of vision, affecting the observer. The Chapel's graffiti, and its wall-paintings, had an affective power and both were designed and invested with meanings understood by the medieval audience that are hard for the modern viewer to appreciate.

Medieval manuscripts also contain astrological charts and horoscopes (maps of the heavens) consisting of concentric circles which represent the celestial spheres or orbs on which the stars and planets were fixed as they rotated the earth. Some graffiti might relate to medieval astrology. Medieval astrologers thought there was a symmetry between the stars and planets and events on earth

Figs 23 & 24. Concentric circles under *Erthe upon Erthe*.

and, by tracking them, they believed they could make predictions about a wide range of events from war, pestilence and death, to more mundane matters such as when to plant a crop, get married or the best time to close a business deal. Astrological knowledge permeated all levels of society and was not incompatible with being a Christian: the effect of the heavens on earth was just one more manifestation of God's influence and was an important tool for calculating the Church calendar for any given year.

Fig. 25. Compass wheel, north wall, under layers of post-Reformation paint. *Image: Rodger Palmer.*

Fig. 26. Concentric circles behind glass, upper rooms, Guildhall.

Now behind glass in the upper rooms of Stratford's Guildhall, there is a superb set of concentric circles which looks as if it may have had an astrological purpose (fig. 26). The circles are carved onto the fifteenth-century plasterwork which was hidden behind a fireplace for over a hundred years before being revealed in 1949. The upper floor of the Guildhall was probably used for the sorts of meetings and feasts the Guild had previously held in the Chapel, while the lower floor housed the chaplains' rooms and a small chapel.

There are also compass wheels on the medieval timber window frames in the upper Guildhall, their location suggesting they had an apotropaic function (fig. 27).

Fig. 27. Compass wheel, window frame, upper rooms, Guildhall.

Returning to the south-west corner of the Chapel, there is a row of three small overlapping circles carved into the stonework (fig. 28). Such circles appear frequently in churches in apotropaic contexts, sometimes strung together in rows or clusters in far greater numbers than in the Chapel. They may have been carved with a rase knife, a U-shaped scribing tool usually used by carpenters to mark-up components of timber frames.

3. Medieval graffiti

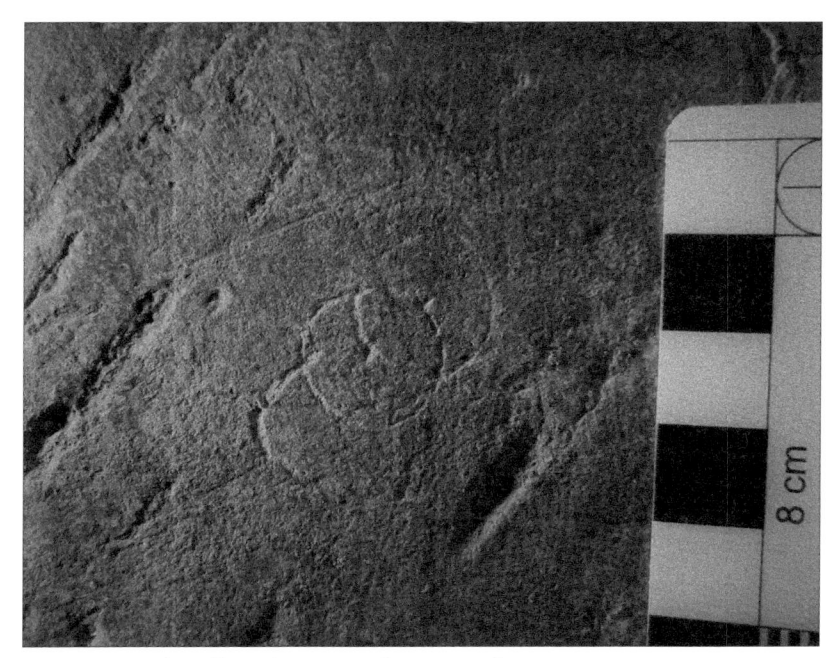

Fig. 28. Row of small overlapping circles, west wall.

Fig. 29. Large compass wheel, east wall, north porch.

A common location for compass-drawn graffiti is the porch, clearly a place where evil spirits could enter the building. Despite the poor quality of the stonework in the porch of the Guild Chapel, there are hints of at least three compass wheels, the largest on the east wall of the porch, near the inner door (fig. 29). It has a deep central point, possibly where the point of the implement dug into the wall, and may have consisted of additional concentric circles.

After the Reformation, as the Church began to view them as superstitious, ritual protection marks, especially compass wheels, began to appear increasingly in domestic buildings where they are often found on beams and fireplaces. A single compass-drawn design has survived in Anne Hathaway's Cottage in Shottery, a mile from Stratford, where Shakespeare's wife, Anne (nee Hathaway), grew up. The graffito is on a beam in the extension of the house and the Shakespeare Birthplace Trust suggests it was carved very soon after the extension was completed in the early-1600s. The symbol is positioned centrally in the room, on the beam which extends at right angles from the fireplace, roughly midway between the windows on either side of the room. The room also has two doors opening off it. Ritual protection marks are often positioned between vulnerable portals in this way.

In Nash's House, the house next door to New Place that once belonged to Shakespeare's grandson-in-law, Thomas Nash, a complex pattern of rosettes was recorded on one of the timbers by the cellar, probably beside a lost doorway. Again, a date in the early-1600s has been proposed. Ritual protection marks tend to survive better in cellars as they are subject to less alteration than other areas of a building.

At the top of the cellar stairs in Shakespeare's Birthplace in Henley Street in Stratford, there are two well-preserved rosettes (fig. 30). The Birthplace Trust dates them to about 1600 when the house was leased to a publican and the rear of the property was extended and converted into a tavern. It is said the rosettes may have been added by the publican to protect the cellar and the precious beer stored there. Compass wheel graffiti is commonly found in barns and wherever valuable livestock was housed.

There is another example of threshold protection on the fireplace next to the cellar stairs. On the timber mantel is a set of burn marks with the classic tear-shaped scorching typical of apotropaic burn marks (fig. 31). Such burn marks are common around fireplaces – open and vulnerable to fire, they needed more protection. Burn marks seem to stem from concerns that witches might be setting fire to buildings; the marks 'inoculated' the area against them, effectively fighting fire with fire. If you touched the wood with a flame, accidental or malicious fire would somehow be prevented.

Fig. 30. Compass wheels in Shakespeare's Birthplace.

Fig. 31. Burn marks, fireplace, Shakespeare's Birthplace.

As with other ritual protection marks, it is difficult to date burn marks, but the addition of protective markings often followed the insertion of a chimney into an existing building as the integrity of the structure was deemed to have been broken. Burn marks are evident on other mantel beams within Shakespeare's Birthplace.

Experimentation has proved that these burn marks were not accidental; they seem to have been a very deliberate ritual practice. They were not limited to fireplaces and have been found on the woodwork of churches and throughout domestic settings in roof spaces, stairs, around windows and on doors. Burn marks have been documented in the roof-space of Shakespeare's Birthplace. There is also a burn mark midway between two windows in the kitchen of Anne Hathaway's Cottage in part of the original 1463 house, perhaps marking a boundary in some way as well as offering protection. Burn marks might be linked in the medieval mind to the spiritual power of light and candles, but it is clear they had some sort of apotropaic function, the chimney was simply considered the area most at risk. Maybe today's superstition that touching wood brings good luck stems from the medieval practice of making burn marks?

Lightning Strikes

While many ritual protection marks seem to embody the traditional views and beliefs of the typical medieval churchgoer, others appear to reflect folklore and superstition at the margins of medieval society. In fact, all markings were firmly embedded in everyday church life and used by all levels of society. An intriguing little graffito on the tower arch of the Guild Chapel is a small zig-zag, measuring three centimetres in height (fig. 32). Zig-zag motifs, which can often look like little more than haphazard scratches, have been interpreted as lightning strikes and a defence against thunderstorms which people believed were caused by demons. Lightning was a very real threat in the days of timber-framed buildings and thatched rooves.

The zig-zag in the Chapel is thought to be a lightning strike rather than a mason's mark as it does not appear to have been made with a chisel and is not as neat and well-executed as masons' marks tend to be (fig. 7). Carving such symbols was an attempt by individuals to control their environment and maybe the one in the Chapel brought some comfort to Guild members that they might '*fear no more the lightning flash*' (Shakespeare, *Cymbeline*, act 4, scene 2).

Lightning-strike graffiti is frequently found on rood screens, which were often made from oak timbers. Oak timbers were thought to have an immunity from lightning, especially if they were from a tree that had already been struck – it is probably how we get the saying 'lightning never strikes twice in the same place'. Rood screens were a common place for ritual protection marks, probably because they represented another threshold. It is not known what ultimately happened to the Chapel's rood screen. It was removed in 1641 in order that a pulpit could be conveniently placed (the rood loft and rood had been removed in 1564-65). Some of the panels from the screen were then used at the west end of the Chapel and survived until the mid-twentieth century refurbishments.[9]

Fig. 32. Lightning strike, tower arch. *Image: Terry Galvin.*

It is almost impossible to precisely date a graffito such as the Chapel's lightning strike, and its purpose might have been quite different to the one attributed to it. If it is a lightning strike, its location may be significant as the archway leads to the bell tower. Bells were blessed when installed and believed to be spiritual objects with the power to bless anyone in earshot. In addition to calling people to church, they frightened away evil spirits before the congregation assembled below.

---

9   A report in the Victoria County History for Warwickshire, dated 1945, describes the panels from the rood screen as having 'moulded posts on which are small shafts with moulded octagonal caps. The heads of the lights are mostly subcusped cinquefoiled arches with rosette cusp-points'.

From about the thirteenth century onwards, people began to think that the ringing of the church bell would also drive away the demons which caused lightning, so bells were ritually rung during thunderstorms to calm the storm. The practice persisted well into the modern period, often with terrible consequences for the bell-ringers: a church tower was not the best place to be in a storm. New bells were recorded in the Guild accounts for 1442-43 and there was work done on them in 1471-72. They survived the Reformation and were repaired again, recast and rehung at various times between 1582 and 1633. The 'Great Bell' of 1633 was renovated in 2018 and once again chimes the hour and rings the curfew at eight o'clock every night, warning Stratfordians to dampen their hearths to prevent unattended fires burning out of control. The bell would ring again in the morning to let people know they could re-light their fires. The familiar ringing of the Chapel bells would have regulated the lives of William Shakespeare and his family while they resided at New Place; whether the bells were a comforting sound or an annoying intrusion, the Shakespeares could hardly have failed to hear them.

Marks like lightning strikes have been carved onto the oak and elm standing desk currently in the upper rooms of the Guildhall, which tradition claims is Shakespeare's desk (figs 33 and 34). It has been dated to the fifteenth or sixteenth century, although there are later patches and additions, doubtless necessitated by relic-hunters taking souvenirs.

Fig. 33. Oak and elm standing desk, Guildhall.

3. Medieval graffiti

Fig. 34. 'Lightning strike', desk, upper rooms, Guildhall.

Did a 'lightning flash' cause the fire in the poorhouses built by the Guild? The Guild accounts for 1413-14 record that money was received for '*burnt timber of two poorhouses after the fire*'. It was after the fire that the Guild took the opportunity to build the new Guildhall, on the site of the destroyed poorhouses (fig. 35).

Fig. 35. The Guildhall with the adjoining Chapel in the background.

Ladders and chequer-board designs

There is a wide assortment of markings that might have been considered apotropaic. Like lightning-strike graffiti, ladder motifs are also thought to be significant, symbolising salvation and the climbing away from evil. Also common are chequer-board designs, and graffiti with a ladder-like or chequer-board appearance has been found on the Chapel's chancel arch on the south side (fig. 36). Exactly what the function or meaning of chequer-board graffiti was is unclear - the criss-crossing lines may have been designed to pin evil spirits to the wall in the same way as compass wheels. The examples on the chancel arch, while faint, are distinctive. Unfortunately, they are difficult to photograph owing to the concave surface and the fact they are behind a wooden hymn board fixed to the wall!

Fig. 36. Ladder-like/chequer-board inscriptions on the chancel arch, carved across several of the stone blocks.

Merels

There are many symbols and pictures whose meanings may always remain unknown, the original intent of the inscriber, long forgotten. An example in the Chapel is the small graffito on the south door surround (fig. 37). It has remnants of paint in its grooves. There is no agreement on what it might mean, but it is in the same context as other ritual protection marks so may have had a similar purpose.

Fig. 37. South door surround, nave. Size H. 6cm.

The graffito by the south door looks similar to the merels that are so widespread in churches (fig. 38). It is certainly in an area in the Chapel where there are a significant number of merels and other ritual protection marks. They are called merels because they look like the ancient game, Merels, or Nine-Men's-Morris, a strategy game for two people, played on a square board with marked, fixed points.

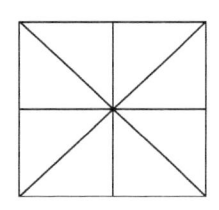

Fig. 38. Three-Men's-Morris type merel.

Nine-Men's-Morris was a popular game in medieval England and related to it were Three-, Six-, and Twelve-Men's-Morris. It is a game Shakespeare was familiar with. In *A Midsummer Night's Dream,* Titania laments that '*the nine men's morris is fill'd up with mud*' (act 2, scene 1). A Nine-Men's-Morris was marked out in the grass by the theatre in Stratford in the early-1900s in much the same way that the fictional Titania's might have been.

The similarity of graffiti merels to the games has led some people to dismiss them as merely small versions of the games. The problem with this is they are often found in religious buildings and on vertical surfaces where they are unplayable; the high incidence of them in non-playable contexts suggests something else is going on. Although no one knows exactly what the meaning and function of merels was, like many ritual protection symbols, they are often clustered together and found amongst or near marks recognised as apotropaic. Merels also have elements that are characteristic of symbols that are thought to be protective, so it is reasonable to think they had the same purpose. The Three-Men's-Morris type is by far the most common graffiti version and it is this form that is found in the Chapel, all of them on vertical surfaces. One of the best examples in the Chapel is on the base of a pillar on the tower arch (fig. 39). It is situated low down so probably carved from a kneeling or sitting position.

Fig. 39. Merel, tower arch, west wall, north side. H. 7cm.

By carving merels onto consecrated walls there may have been a perception that this would enhance their power. Were they another attempt to pin evil spirits to the wall or prevent them from entering a building? Amongst the magical diagrams found in medieval manuscripts are squares containing what look like X-shaped crosses; these were used by magicians to protect against conjured spirits. Perhaps merels evolved from these magical diagrams? Merels also look like illustrations in medieval manuscripts associated with astrology and making horoscopes so this might be another explanation. Maybe they derive from the eight-armed baptismal cross?

The meaning and function of merels may have changed over time and are dependent upon the context in which they were created. Undoubtedly some merels will be gaming boards. There are merels on the standing desk in the Guildhall and on the horizontal surface of the marble table-tomb of the wool merchant, Richard Hill (d.1593), in the St Peter Chapel in Holy Trinity Church and these two examples may well be games. We should perhaps find another name for the symbols in churches to distinguish them from simple gaming boards such as these.

Fig. 40. Merel, tower arch. *Image: Rodger Palmer.*

The south west corner of the Chapel has several merels. There is another example on the tower arch not far from the merel we have already seen (fig. 40). There is also a merel on the south wall (fig. 41) and one on the west wall (fig. 42). Ritual protection marks are often found in clusters around openings, opposite doors and equidistant between doors and windows. The concentration of ritual protection marks on the archway leading to the tower and in the west end of the nave suggests that this area was considered particularly vulnerable to penetration by evil spirits. The tower alone was a portal that would have caused considerable concern, and the tower arch was midpoint between the openings of the north, south and west doors.

Unlike the merels on the tower arch which must have been inscribed by someone kneeling or sitting, the merel located on the south wall is above eye-level, another indication that they are unlikely to be small versions of a game (fig. 41).

Fig. 41. Merel, south wall, right of the south door.

The merel on the tower arch (fig. 39) is criss-crossed with lines. Close examination suggests the criss-crossing lines were scored over the top of the merel, begging the questions why and when. The general tendency is that individual graffiti were not drawn over, they were left intact and overlap was avoided. It might have been deliberately scored over, perhaps after the Reformation when ritual protection marks came to be viewed as superstitious, or maybe it was hidden beneath paint when the lines were added. Similar to chequer-board patterns, criss-crossed lines or mesh patterns are thought to be another form

3. Medieval graffiti

of ritual protection, the intention again, perhaps, to trap evil spirits in the lines or pin them to the wall. There is cross-hatching scored all around the base of the pillars on the north side of the tower arch. Again, it has proved difficult to photograph owing to the curvature of the stone blocks (fig. 43).

Fig. 42. Merel, west wall; it is unclear if it was carved before *Erthe upon Erthe* was painted.

Fig. 43. Cross-hatching, tower arch, west wall.

45

Butterfly marks

Inscriptions known as butterfly marks, or butterfly crosses, are another common symbol and appear regularly on stone and woodwork. They look like two triangles meeting at a point and resemble a bow-tie. Some, undoubtedly, will be masons' marks or, when inscribed on timber, carpenters' laying out marks. However, a large number are found in situations where it is unlikely a workman would have inscribed them, on fonts for example, suggesting they may have had some other purpose. They are often seen amongst other apotropaic marks near openings in buildings.

Although it is similar to some of the masons' marks in the Chapel (fig. 9), a mark on the door surround in the north wall might be a butterfly cross rather than a mason's mark (fig. 44). It is not as neatly executed as might be expected for a mason's mark and does not appear to have been created using a chisel. Also, its presence on the door surround, amongst other ritual protection marks, might indicate it had a similar meaning or function.

Fig. 44. Butterfly mark, door surround, north wall. *Image: Rodger Palmer.*

There is evidence of another butterfly mark on the chancel arch. This mark is very faint so much harder to see, but, again, it does not appear to have been created with a chisel. There is also a butterfly mark on the plasterwork in the Guildhall.

Butterfly symbols, like other protection marks, may have ancient origins and are found all over the world. Various interpretations have been attached to them. One suggestion is that the symbol stems from the Saxon runic alphabet. Alternatively, the British Museum has suggested similar symbols were being used in early Christian Nubia (central Sudan) where, it is thought, the symbol was a monogram representing the Greek form of the name Michael. It is possible the symbol filtered across Christendom and was linked to the once popular cult of Saint Michael, forming the root of the butterfly cross now recognised as apotropaic, surviving in folk memory, even if its original meaning was long forgotten.[10]

Fig. 45. Carpenters' levelling mark.

Butterfly marks may have evolved from masons' marks or carpenters' construction marks (fig. 45). It is possible people copied the marks, not necessarily knowing why, but they sensed they had to make the building 'right' somehow and the marks came to have an apotropaic function. It is still used as a construction mark; there is one in the Chapel's roof space drawn in ochre chalk, probably left when the new ceiling was fitted.

Dot patterns

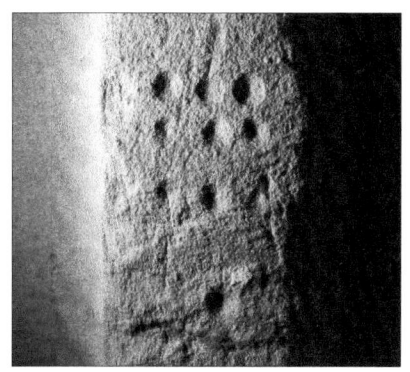

Fig. 46. Dot pattern, door surround, inner door, porch.

Fig. 47. Dot pattern, door surround, north wall.

Dot patterns are another puzzling but regular manifestation in churches, and the Chapel has some good examples in the north porch and around the north door (figs 46 and 47). Generally, dot patterns

---

10 It is thought the feathered angel in the Chapel's *Erthe upon Erthe* painting is the Archangel Michael (fig. 58).

are deeply inscribed and often grouped together. Many dot clusters have a numerical value. They are frequently uneven and bunched in groups of three, five, seven and nine. In medieval Christianity, numbers could have a powerful religious or mystical significance: three was used extensively as a symbol of the Trinity; five symbolized the five wounds of Christ at his crucifixion; there were seven sacraments, and seven appears repeatedly through the Bible associated with perfection; nine dots might symbolize the Trinity three times over, the number of the angels since there are nine choirs of them, or even represent the novena prayers which are carried out over nine consecutive days. The number eight, through the octagon, is a symbol of Jesus, unifying God and earth.[11] Numbers were also used in divination and medieval magic so they may have represented some sort of code.

Fig. 48. Dot pattern, Holy Trinity, Stratford-upon-Avon.

It is possible some dots once traced patterns or images painted onto the surface of walls, so some dot patterns may be all that is left of less deeply incised lettering or images. Very little graffiti has survived inside nearby Holy Trinity Church, but, on a vertical surface in the porch, there is a pattern of dots which seems to have formed the terminals for a star or flower, or even a merel (fig. 48).[12] The example in the porch of Holy Trinity may be incomplete or damaged as, in its current form, it appears to have only seven spokes rather than the usual eight spokes of merels and baptismal crosses.

Dots were routinely used as terminus points for stars, crosses, initials and so on. On the chancel arch are the letters TC or I/JC (fig. 49). There does not appear to be a date.

---

11 An octagon is halfway between a circle (God) and a square (Jesus); just as Jesus was the incarnation of God on earth, so the octagon mediates between the two. Fonts and pulpits are often octagonal - heaven and earth combine during baptism and, during a sermon, the preacher communicates the word of God.

12 The external east wall of Holy Trinity Church is covered with some wonderful graffiti inscriptions dating from the seventeenth to the twenty-first century; the graffiti consists mostly of dated names and initials but there is the odd mark that looks as if it might have been protective.

Fig. 49. Initials with dot terminals, chancel arch, north side.

Dot patterns may be the result of folk medicine rather than specifically apotropaic. It is not clear if people held similar beliefs in England, but in France, until fairly recently, it was believed that drilling holes into church walls, which were considered holy, and mixing the resulting powder with wine, produced a cure for all ills. If the dots were arranged in patterns with religious significance, this may have doubled the spiritual potency of the act. Dot patterns may have contained elements of some or all of the ideas explored here.

Merchants' marks

On the surround of the south door is a mark that could be mistaken for a mason's mark (fig. 50). It does appear as if it might have started out as one - three of the lines at the base look as though they were made with a chisel. It actually has the appearance of a merchant's mark, a distinctive symbol or 'signature' used by merchants in numerous ways: to mark goods and property, sign documents, on personal seals and so on. They are often found incorporated into stained-glass windows to record who paid for them, on monumental brasses and gravestones as well as in decorative features in domestic settings. There was a huge variety of merchants' marks and they were instantly recognisable, to both the literate and illiterate, as belonging to a particular individual and could be handed down to later generations (fig. 51).

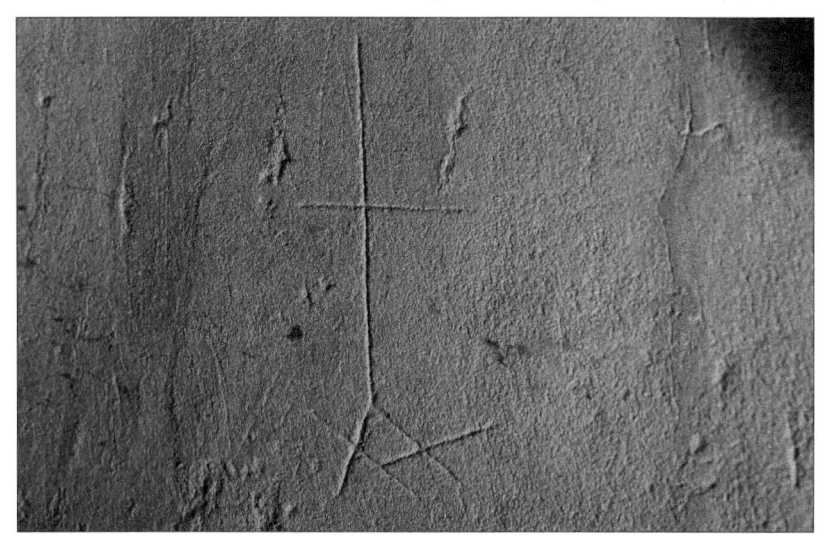

Fig. 50. Large mark, door surround, south door, nave.

Merchants' marks are often mistaken for masons' marks as they are similar in style and structure, although merchants' marks tend to be bigger and less neatly drawn than masons' marks and are far more likely to contain curved elements including lettering. At ten centimetres in height, the mark in the Chapel is considerably larger than any of the Chapel's masons' marks. It is also similar to merchants' marks seen elsewhere.

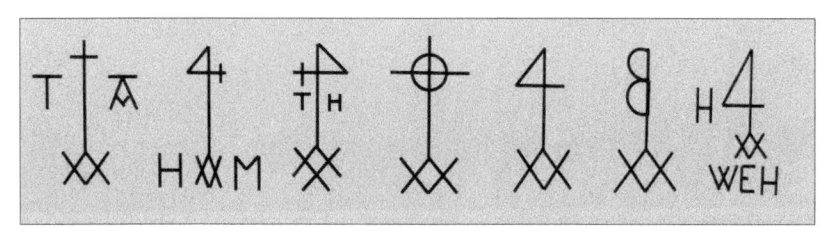

Fig. 51. Examples of merchants' marks from various locations.

The Chapel's mark is on its own, high up on the surround of the south door of the nave and merchants' marks are often found isolated in this location. They can also be found clustered in areas which might have had a particular significance. There is a cluster of merchants' marks carved onto the medieval stalls in the vestibule of the Dean's Chapel in the Collegiate Church of St Mary in Warwick. Merchants' marks are also common in church porches where business transactions were completed and a mark, the same as the one in the Chapel, has been seen amongst merchants' marks in the porch of the church of St Mary the Virgin, in Kenardington in Kent. Carving what was, in effect, a business logo onto the consecrated walls of a church was a form of advertising, but it also suggests a desire for divine sanction for the individual concerned and whatever business they were involved in.

Some merchants' marks relate to religious or trade guilds, rather than a particular individual. Those that appear generic with merely a different date or initials are likely to be the symbol of a trade or religious guild. Local guilds would sometimes copy the practice of the larger livery companies in cities like London and Bristol who had their own specialist marks, particularly when the guild was associated with a side altar or guild chapel. Perhaps a member of the Stratford guild wanted to be like these larger livery companies, and copied a mark they had seen while travelling on business. Hugh Clopton, the benefactor who paid for the Chapel to be rebuilt in stone and painted, was apprenticed to the Worshipful Company of Mercers in London around 1454-56, and rose through the ranks of the Company; he became a member in 1463-64 and later served as a warden. Many of the merchants, traders and artisans who belonged to the Guild of the Holy Cross in Stratford would have had similar links with the livery companies of London and other towns and cities. The Guild *Register* reveals that members increasingly came from further afield during the fifteenth century.

When offering interpretations of historic graffiti, it is all too easy to ascribe constructs to it that were never intended. Unfortunately, we may never know for sure what this mark was intended to be. All we can say with any certainty is that it looks like a mason's mark that was subsequently enlarged and altered for some reason, and that similar marks have been seen elsewhere that might suggest it is a merchant's mark.

Another possible merchant's mark can be found on the Chapel's chancel arch (fig. 52). Here, the initials AB are carved several times and, at first glance, they appear to be just that, simply initials. However, a closer look reveals the '4' typical of so many merchants' marks (fig. 53). It is strikingly similar to a merchant's mark in St. Mary's Church in Warwick. According to the Guild *Register*, there were a number of Guild members from Warwick, including canons from St Mary's Church who joined the Stratford guild in the late-fifteenth century.

Fig. 52. Chancel arch, south side.

Fig. 53. Detail highlighting the '4' typical of merchants' marks.

Heraldry

Shields, coats of arms and heraldic symbols are relatively common. Some can be intricately carved full coats of arms whilst others are basic outlines. It is difficult to identify specific families even where they are well-executed as heraldry relies on colour, without which a single shield could potentially belong to a dozen families or more.

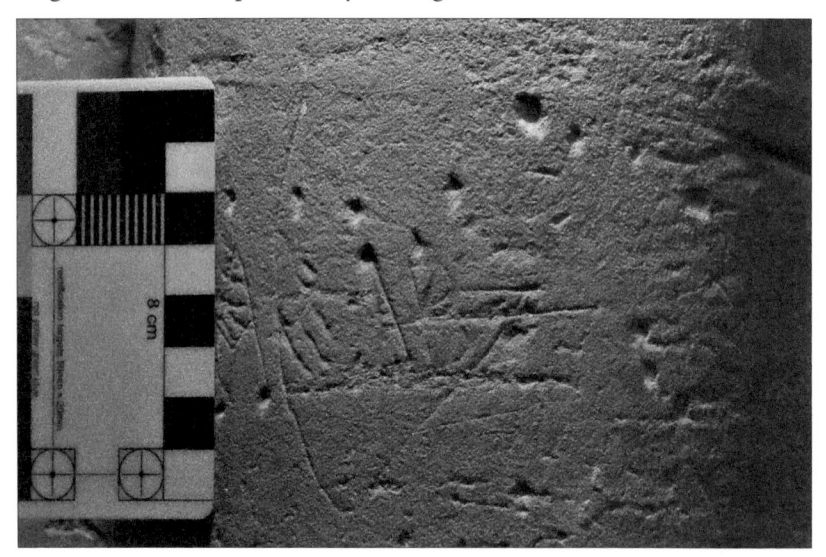

Fig. 54. Shield, chancel arch, north side. *Image: Rodger Palmer.*

Interestingly, heraldic graffiti was the most likely to be defaced, probably because it related to a particular individual. Defacing it was an effective way of insulting someone and might even have had the more sinister intention of invoking misfortune on the individuals concerned. Graffiti of a devotional nature was less likely to be attacked for fear it would bring the wrath of God down on the perpetrator.

3. Medieval graffiti

On the chancel arch on the north side of the Guild Chapel is a shield which appears to contain the initials AB (fig. 54). It is unclear whether AB was originally part of the shield. Is this AB the same AB who left his initials and possible merchant's mark on the other side of the chancel arch (fig. 52)? The graffiti shield may have been positioned to use the colours on the walls to replicate the colours of the heraldry, something that is seen on the continent.

Perhaps whoever drew the shield in the Chapel aspired to have a coat of arms like Hugh Clopton and other Guild elites? The medieval stained glass within the Chapel would probably have featured the heraldry of benefactors and influential families. The once painted wooden angels that stood amongst the foliage bosses on the medieval timber roof would also have carried coats of arms (fig. 55). Maybe the shield was carved at a much later date by someone emulating William Shakespeare and his father, who were finally awarded a coat of arms in 1596 and likely displayed their shield proudly above the entrance to New Place?

Fig. 55. Medieval wooden angel from the Guild Chapel.

A closer look at the shield reveals another very distinct A to its left (fig. 56). It is similar to the lettering around the merchant's mark on the chancel arch (fig. 52). The broken-bar A's in the Chapel are not masons' marks, but they are reminiscent of the masonic symbol of a square overlaid with a pair of compasses. On the pillars in the nave of Holy Trinity Church in Stratford, there are numerous broken bar A-shapes. These are masons' marks. The pillars in question date from the 1300s.

Fig. 56. Close-up of the shield. *Image: Rodger Palmer.*

Some broken-bar A's might be an integrated M and A. The MA symbol has been found amongst apotropaic graffiti, often in conjunction with VV and M symbols and, like them, is also associated with the Virgin Mary.

Fig. 57. MARIA monogram

The broken-bar A is sometimes seen with two additional lines to make a combined MAR, supporting the theory that it has a Marian derivation. If the straight line of the MAR is treated as the letter I, the grouping could represent the name MARIA. Such symbols can be seen from the late-1500s and as late as the end of the 1600s. As time went on, broken bar A's may have lost their association with the Virgin Mary and become simply an elaborate version of the letter.

Text inscriptions

There is a short piece of writing inscribed onto the west wall underneath the painting, *Erthe upon Erthe*, dating it to the late-1490s (figs 58 and 59). The style of the script also suggests it is from this period. It is indecipherable - medieval graffiti inscriptions are notoriously hard to read as not only are they frequently worn or incomplete, they are often in Latin. Sometimes it is only possible to identify it as text and recognise the odd letter. In a lovely coincidence, the left hand of the figure on the right, possibly a female member of a burial party, seems to be pointing directly at the text.

******

In medieval churches and cathedrals everywhere, there are myriad graffiti images of people, faces, hands and feet, ships, animals, birds, fish, musical notes, musical instruments, armed men – foot soldiers as well as knights and archers - along with an array of the weaponry they might have used, charms and curses not to mention pictures of demons and the odd dragon, all of which warrant conservation. The original meaning and significance of many remain unknown. Some of the images are apotropaic, or appear to have been drawn from biblical stories, others may have been based on the imagery of pilgrim badges and pilgrim souvenirs which were popular in the medieval period, but for many, without hard evidence, it is only possible to offer the most likely interpretation or theory as to what they might have meant.

3. Medieval graffiti

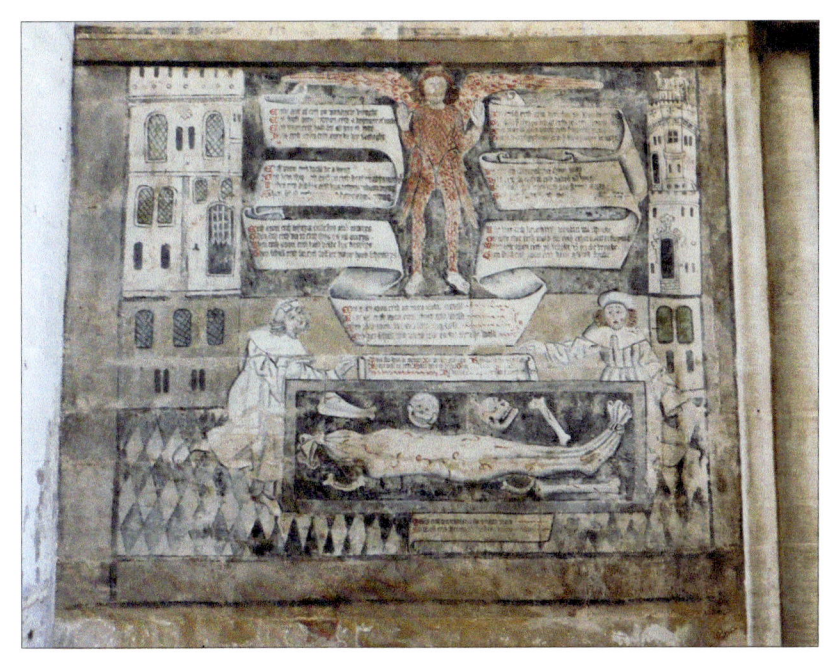

Fig. 58. *Erthe upon Erthe*, an allegory on death.

Fig. 59. Detail showing the script.

Figs 60-63. Clockwise: dagger, the Abbey, Holyroodhouse, Edinburgh; hand, All Saints' Church, Litcham, Norfolk; face, Bedingfeld Chapel, Oxborough, Norfolk; ship graffiti at St Andrews, Blickling, Norfolk.

Is there more graffiti behind the twentieth-century panelling that still covers the *Dance of Death* painting on the north wall, the *Lyf of Adam* on the south wall and the painting on the lower west wall of the Chapel? At sites in Britain and across Europe, there are examples of graffiti inscriptions actually tracing the images in wall-paintings. People were encouraged and even expected to physically interact with the formal paint scheme. Graffiti was just one more element in the rich and vibrant 'multimedia' experience that was the medieval church, which was filled with texts, images, and the music, sounds and smells of religious life. Despite the looming presence of death and judgement painted on the walls, attendance at mass was a social occasion, an opportunity for laughter, entertainment and trade as people came together with their friends, acquaintances and business contacts, the familiar devotional images on the walls, in the windows and sculptures, all forming part of their religious community. There would have been ample opportunity to draw on the walls before fixed pews and benches became standard church furniture. Before the Reformation, there was little seating and an emphasis on 'seeing' the mass. After the Reformation, attendance at church became a much more static experience as Protestantism prioritised the word of God and 'listening' became central to worship. Pews were fitted in the Guild Chapel in 1564-65, about the time the Chapel became a preaching venue, reflecting these changing priorities.

Despite Henry VIII's break with Rome, there was little material change to most churches during his reign. Under his son, Edward VI (1547-1553), however, the changes were sweeping and as part of his reforms, all religious guilds were dissolved (closed). In the 1550s, following the dissolution of the Stratford guild in 1547, it is likely the Guild Chapel was shut and locked, the building more or less liturgically redundant and probably viewed as little more than prime real estate. There would have been limited opportunities to draw on the walls now.

Edward's religious legislation brought an end to centuries of belief and tradition, undermining the social structures of medieval England. Catholics saw a large part of their belief system outlawed at a stroke by an Act of Parliament that summarily declared purgatory did not exist. Prayers for the dead were no longer needed, the worshipping and adoration of images and relics was forbidden, and the invocation of saints banned. In Stratford, the loss of the once powerful Guild must have had a profound effect. Not only was the Guild's beloved Chapel now defunct and its religious purpose terminated, its socially cohesive role within the community had come to an end, its possessions were confiscated, and the future of the almshouses and school were threatened. While the influence of religious guilds in general had been waning as a result of religious uncertainties and efforts by the Government to curb their power, it must have been deeply unsettling. We only have to look at the Guild *Register* in the period before the Guild was closed to know that people still found the idea of intercessionary prayer convincing - after 1515 new membership was increasingly for the souls of the already deceased.

Key figures within the Guild did retain some influence. Most of those involved in Stratford's petition to Edward VI for a licence of incorporation and the return of the Guild and College property, including the Chapel, had previously played a leading part in Guild affairs. A Royal Charter was granted in 1553 in the last week of Edward VI's reign and the new Corporation continued many of the roles previously played by the Guild. Under Queen Mary mass was occasionally said in the Chapel, but, with the accession of Elizabeth I, these were abandoned and, during her reign, there was only a non-compulsory weekly sermon. In the decades after Shakespeare was born, the initially conservative Corporation increasingly conformed to the Elizabethan settlement.

4. After the Reformation

THE CHAPEL AND ITS GRAFFITI IN THE YEARS AFTER SHAKESPEARE'S BIRTH

Such was the Guild Chapel on the eve of William Shakespeare's birth. He was born in 1564 as the old world was giving way to the new. Change was gradual in rural settlements like Stratford-upon-Avon and religious ideas were slow to change after the Reformation. People may have been told what religion to follow but they did not forget old beliefs easily; while the half of the population who saw the Catholic Church as corrupt may have welcomed the religious reforms of the sixteenth century, the other half were likely horrified by it.

The physical appearance of the Chapel probably changed little until the mid-1560s, despite Edward VI's legislation and Queen Elizabeth's subsequent 1559 injunction demanding the removal of *'all signs of superstition and idolatry'* from places of worship. The late removal of anything 'Catholic' from the Guild Chapel may have been an active resistance to Protestant reforms but, equally, it may have been the result of a pragmatic desire to keep unnecessary costs down for a building that was little used.

William Shakespeare's father, John, was chamberlain (treasurer) for Stratford Corporation when the paintings in the Chapel were whitewashed in 1563. It is not known how he felt about it, but he and his colleagues were responsible for this first recorded act of iconoclasm. He noted the payment of two shillings (ten pence) in the town accounts for the lime pails and brushes *'for defasyng ymages in ye chappell'* shortly before his son, William, was born. John Shakespeare had risen quickly from humble beginnings, the highpoint of his career coming in 1568 when he was appointed bailiff (mayor). For a while, he had both wealth and influence before he was targeted by professional informers and charged with usury and illegal wool dealing, crimes he was almost certainly guilty of. The legal actions brought against John Shakespeare until at least 1583 destroyed his business career; he gradually withdrew from public life and in 1586 he was finally dismissed from his post on the council after repeatedly missing meetings.

Just a thin layer of whitewash was applied to the walls of the Chapel in 1563, perhaps so the paintings could be revealed again at some point. After years of religious turmoil, nobody could have known if or how things might change again. A cursory whitewashing was probably all that could be done in a couple of days – a payment of two shillings represents about two days' work for a less-skilled workman. The shadows of the paintings and graffiti alike may well have shown through, and in a damp church it would have been easy to dry-brush the whitewash off, leaving residues in the grooves of the graffiti, highlighting it. There is evidence the *Dance of Death* painting on the north wall of the nave may have escaped the first whitewashing in 1563-64, possibly because it was considered less troublesome than more explicitly religious paintings. Any graffiti scratched onto it would have remained clearly visible, the pale stone beneath standing out. Even on the walls that were whitewashed, some of the more deeply-carved graffiti may still have been discernible. The walls in the nave were whitewashed again in 1586-87, finally obliterating any remnants of the paintings there and probably much of the medieval graffiti too.

The medieval association of images and objects with a protective function persisted long after Protestantism deemed them to be superstitious, and people continued to believe in the protective nature of apotropaic graffiti - such ingrained beliefs did not disappear overnight. Even though the Protestant Reformation tried to take the magic out of religion, witchcraft, astrology, divination and all kinds of popular magic thrived in England in the sixteenth and seventeenth centuries. Shakespeare's plays reflect these continuing beliefs and superstitions. *Macbeth, Hamlet* and *A Midsummer Night's Dream*, for example, explore the themes of heaven and hell, good and evil, witches, demons, fairies and ghosts. Audiences would have taken the witches in *Macbeth* seriously, and seeing the harm they caused in the play probably exacerbated fears of the damage they could inflict in real life. *Macbeth* was most likely written in 1606 about the time the European witch trials were reaching their peak. In 1597, the year William Shakespeare bought New Place, James VI of Scotland (later James I of England) wrote *Daemonologie*, a book about the dangers witches posed and their ability to enter any house or church '*by whatsoever open[ing] the air may enter in at …*'.

We will probably never know if Shakespeare visited the Chapel and saw the graffiti there, but if he did, he would have understood it and accepted it as a normal part of life, perhaps finding comfort in the symbols we still see today, and even carving some of his own. Graffiti was a shorthand for the everyday beliefs and superstitions prevalent in the Stratford into which he had been born, and given the Chapel's proximity to both the grammar school and New Place, he would have known the building well. John Shakespeare's position as bailiff would have given him a key and ready access to the building. He would also have hosted theatrical troupes next door in the Guildhall, the earliest in 1568 when William was four, and it is reasonable to assume he took his son with him. Later, despite his increasingly dire financial situation, John paid for a lavish funeral for his daughter, Anne, who died aged 7 years and 6 months in 1579. In addition to the funeral, John paid 8d for the use of the Chapel pall so that his daughter would '*have with holy bell been knoll'd to church*' (Shakespeare, *As You Like It*, act 2, scene 7). The distraught family would almost certainly have processed past the Chapel with her body on their way to Holy Trinity Church, where William Shakespeare and the rest of his family were later buried alongside her.

It is conceivable that William Shakespeare had his first lessons in the Guild Chapel. There is evidence of a 'petty school' in the Chapel until at least 1594 - a council minute for that year instructs there shall be no school kept in the Chapel '*from this tyme following*'.[13] The petty school would have provided elementary education for local children aged five to seven before the boys progressed to the grammar school next door in the old Guildhall. The grammar school and schoolmaster, once paid for by the Guild, was now financed by Stratford Corporation. The provision of education was a condition of Edward VI's 1553 Charter, and the school was named *The King's New School*.[14] As the son of a town official, Shakespeare's place at the town's free school was almost guaranteed. Over the years, many stories and theories have been advanced about Shakespeare. Writing in London, the seventeenth-century biographer, John Aubrey, suggested that Shakespeare was '*in his younger yeares a school master in the countrey*'. Money was allocated each year for an usher or assistant at the grammar school and it is possible he helped out there, but he may also have helped out at the petty school in the Chapel.

---
13 A council minute in 1628 notes again that there shall be no 'common school' kept in the Chapel.
14 It was subsequently renamed the King Edward VI Grammar School.

As the owner of New Place, Shakespeare would have divided his time between London and Stratford. Although he owned property in London, he was probably only ever a lodger there - his home was in the town where he grew up. New Place was still the largest house in the borough and Shakespeare substantially remodelled it. Renaissance detailing advertised a man's classical education, and sixteenth-century gentry believed it was a virtue and even a public duty to display their wealth and status. New Place was the way in which Shakespeare positioned himself in relation to the community he grew up in and it signalled his social ascendancy - surely he would have bought the house intending to spend as much time there as possible, maybe sensing that *'when [he] was at home, [he] was in a better place'* (Shakespeare, *As You Like It*, act 2, scene 4)?

Fig. 64. View of the Chapel from the site of New Place. The hedge roughly marks the boundary of the house.

At the time Shakespeare owned New Place, it was compulsory for Stratfordians to go to the weekly service at Holy Trinity, the local parish church, or face a fine. Non-compulsory sermons were given at the Chapel while Shakespeare was living at New Place but, again, we will probably never know if he attended any. Living at New Place, he could scarcely have been closer to the familiar haunts of his childhood. While it is hard to discern his religious sympathies from his work, he seems to have known both Protestant teaching and Catholic practice. Wherever Shakespeare's loyalties lay, it is clear the Chapel was a dominant feature in his life, first during his schooldays and then as a writer after 1597. It is not known where in New Place he would have written his plays, but his study, if he had one, was likely set back in the courtyard of the house, perhaps in one of the rooms at one end of the hall, the window facing south to catch the last of the daylight, looking out over the Chapel a few feet away (fig. 64).

Changes in belief and practice brought about by the Reformation were gradual and so were the changes in the content and style of graffiti. Many of the traditional medieval markings persisted, particularly the conjoined-V symbol and compass-drawn designs, although as the Reformation Church became more critical of ritual protection graffiti in churches as the seventeenth century progressed, they transferred to domestic buildings. We have already noted the compass wheels in Shakespeare's Birthplace and Nash's House, and how the conjoined-V continued but slowly became more of a 'good luck' sign. In the same way that apotropaic graffiti gradually transferred to domestic buildings, so did the tradition of storytelling which had played such a fundamental part in worship and instruction before the Reformation. In many surviving early-modern domestic schemes you can see the symbols and stories that were widespread under the Old Faith.

Gradually, graffiti in churches became more secular and memorial in nature – more like the 'I was here' graffiti that we see today. Commemoration and devotional practice had been inextricably linked in the Middle Ages. Individuals had wanted to be remembered after their deaths in order that the prayers of the living would help their souls progress through purgatory. Such beliefs must have been hard to give up and the remnants of those ideas are surely at the root of the memorial graffiti that proliferated in churches from the mid-sixteenth century onwards.

The fact that so much graffiti remains today, both in the Chapel and in religious buildings elsewhere, suggests it was not targeted by zealous reformers in the way that wall-paintings and other iconography were. Less graffiti survives in domestic buildings as their interiors have seen centuries of alterations and this is probably why there is so little in the Shakespeare properties in Stratford. However, graffiti remained widespread and sanctioned in the early-modern period in a way that is entirely alien to us. People had long written on the walls and in the Elizabethan period and beyond, householders continued to do so, the practice being so commonplace as to be unremarkable.

In the Guildhall, next to the Chapel, a list of money spent on salted fish, herrings and cooking oil has been scratched onto the wall in the same way we might casually write a shopping list or menu on a chalk board or white board today (fig. 65). Was this a list of ingredients for one of the Guild's feasts, the fish brought up from the boats that once moored along the River Avon at the bottom of Chapel Lane, the oil bought from the 'Eale Mill' owned by the Guild and from which nearby Ely Street gets its name?

Fig. 65. List of ingredients carved onto the wall of the Guildhall.

In old buildings where the contemporary glass survives, you can still see names and dates etched into the glass. The Reverend Joseph Greene, headmaster of the grammar school (1735–1772), recorded an account from Sir Hugh Clopton (born 1672) after the Clopton family regained possession of New Place in the late-seventeenth century, in which Sir Hugh tells of

'several little epigrams on familiar subjects found upon the glass of the House windows, some of which were written by Shakespeare &

many of them the product of his own children's brain; the tradition being, that he often in his times of pleasantry thus exercis'd his and their talents, and took great pleasure when he could trace in them some petty display of that genius which God & Nature had bless'd himself with'.

Names and initials

There are, inevitably, numerous sets of initials carved into the walls of the Chapel. There is a high incidence of the letter H, inscribed on the chancel arch, in a cluster to the right of the south door in the nave, as well as in the porch. They do not appear to be modern; some are made up of dots and others have dot terminals. One of the most common names in Stratford in the sixteenth and seventeenth centuries was Hamnet, or variations of it. William Shakespeare's close friend and neighbour was Hamnet Sadler, who witnessed Shakespeare's will. Hamnet Sadler and his wife, Judith, were godparents to the infant William and were later godparents to William and Anne Shakespeare's twins, who were named Hamnet and Judith after them. Sadly, Hamnet Shakespeare died in 1596 aged 11.

Fig. 66. Repeated letter H, south door surround.

It is tempting to imagine that some of the H inscriptions might relate to Hamnet Shakespeare - carved perhaps by one of his family or even his father. The family home from 1597 was, after all, just across the lane, and it was common practice for people to scratch their dead children's names onto the consecrated walls of churches, or ask others to do so if they were illiterate. Seeing such inscriptions brings us face-to-face with their grief. Did someone sit on the step of the south door and turn to the wall to mark out in stone their *'griefs unspeakable'* (Shakespeare, *Comedy of Errors*, act 1, scene 1)?

Knowing how the Chapel was being used can help date the graffiti. This, in turn, can shed further light on the Chapel's history. In the 1560s, it seems a wall was constructed between the nave and chancel, and the chancel subsequently subdivided to make multiple compartments. The compartments, which were rented out, were presumably accessed through the priest's door in the chancel. The construction of the wall in the Chapel was a very clear message that, in future, the building's functional use would be prioritised over its religious use. Unfortunately, we do not know exactly where the partition walls were positioned or we might be able to work out when some of the graffiti on the chancel arch was carved. We do know that the wall and chambers would have been *in situ* prior to and during the time Shakespeare was at school and throughout his life afterwards.

From 1562 onwards, the accounts of the Corporation of Stratford record rents from at least five 'chambers' in the Chapel until the mid-seventeenth century when the partitions appear to have been removed. What the chambers were used for is unclear - they may have been living quarters, business units or storage spaces.

RB has been carved several times on the north side of the chancel arch. Whoever RB was he was determined to leave his mark. One set of initials has been deeply carved and has dot terminals (fig. 67). Underneath, RB is written again, this time entirely in dots (fig. 68). Nearby, is a deeply carved RB framed by a square (now partially obscured). None of them is dated. Maybe RB was one of the tenants of the rented chambers? The Corporation accounts suggest that some of them were used as living quarters.

The 1569-70 accounts reveal that one of the tenants, a Richard Burford, paid the sum of ten shillings (approximately £120) for *'A howse rent within the Chapell'*. Burford appears to have been in residence

4. After the Reformation

for some time as the accounts of 1573-74 show rents were still being received from someone of that name. The 1570-71 accounts reveal that a tenant by the name of Richard Binford (possibly Burford misspelt) also paid ten shillings for his *'inhabitacion within the Chapell'*.

Fig. 67. RB, chancel arch, north side, facing east.

Fig. 68. Close-up of the dotted initials RB. *Image: Rodger Palmer.*

The style of the writing suggests the initials are post-Reformation but, in any case, few people would have had access to the chancel before the Reformation when the medieval rood screen was in place (although it was not unknown for members of the medieval church community to carve graffiti). The initials formed from a series of dots are neatly executed and would have taken time to carve. It is impossible to know if the RB who was so keen to carve his initials on the chancel arch was Richard Burford or Richard Binford, but as a tenant of one of the chambers, he would certainly have had the time to carve the letters so deeply and so precisely. In a world where graffiti was still largely tolerated there would have been no need to do it hastily or surreptitiously.

Dots were often used for initials. The practice might hark back to the medieval dot patterns that were thought to have had some sort of protective or magical function. There is another set of initials, WH, created from dots on the chancel arch (fig. 69). It is possible they were carved around the same time as RB.

Fig. 69. WH, chancel arch. *Image: Rodger Palmer.*

Who were RB and WH and what brought them to the Chapel? Attributing initials to someone specific is always problematic. It is slightly easier when you have a full name, but identifying and dating graffiti is never straightforward and it is rarely possible to say conclusively that a particular name belongs to a particular individual, even where there seems to be overwhelming evidence. More often than not, all we can do is speculate.

Clearly inscribed on the chancel arch is the name William Rogers (fig. 70). The inscription is not dated but dates were hardly ever included before the mid-sixteenth century, and only became common in the early-seventeenth century. The style of the writing suggests it could be sixteenth century. The *Register of the Guild of the Holy Cross* records Rogers, Rogger or Roggers from 1428-29 onwards and by the sixteenth century, there were several families with the name Rogers

4. After the Reformation

living in Stratford. There were plenty of men named William Rogers – William was a popular name - but perhaps this graffito belongs to, or was carved in memory of, the William Rogers who lived in Shrieve's House in Sheep Street, a few minutes' walk from the Chapel?

Fig. 70. William Rogers, chancel arch. *Image: Rodger Palmer.*

Fig. 71. Shrieve's House, Sheep Street, Stratford-upon-Avon.

This William Rogers was allegedly a close friend of William Shakespeare. He was a merchant and ran a tavern, but he also served the town in an official capacity as Sergeant at the Mace (Sergeant at Arms). His residence became known as Shrieve's House in the twentieth century, named after William Sheryve, the first recorded tenant in 1542, and archer to Henry VIII (fig. 71). The house once formed part of the substantial property portfolio of the Guild of the Holy Cross. It was rebuilt by William Rogers after a fire in 1595 which destroyed a large part of the town.

Fig. 72. Thomas Rogers, chancel arch. *Image: Rodger Palmer.*

Fig. 73. Thomas Rogers, also on the chancel arch.

4. After the Reformation

Close to the William Rogers graffito on the chancel arch is another name, Thomas Rogers. Did William and Thomas know each other? Thomas, or someone on his behalf, was very keen to record his name in the Chapel as it has been carved twice (figs 72 and 73). Neither is dated but the similarities in style suggest they may have been written by the same person.

Fig. 74. Harvard House, Stratford-upon-Avon.

There was a Thomas Rogers residing in Stratford who was a contemporary of William Rogers and he too was known to Shakespeare as he had served as an alderman with Shakespeare's father. Shakespeare may also have known his son-in-law, Robert Harvard, who lived in Southwark, the heart of the theatrical world in London. Thomas was a wealthy butcher, maltster and grazier, and he rebuilt what later became known as Harvard House on High Street following a fire in 1594 (fig. 74). It was one of Stratford's finest buildings when it was completed. Like Shrieve's House, Harvard House is just a few minutes' walk from the Guild Chapel. The building was named after Thomas Rogers' grandson, John Harvard, a minister who emigrated to America and, upon his death in 1638, bequeathed his library of 400 books and half his estate to what was then Cambridge University but was later renamed Harvard University.

Perhaps William and Thomas were seeking some sort of spiritual reconnection in a place that still had meaning to them? Did they feel unsettled by the devastating fires of 1594 and 1595, and see them as a warning from God? Both fires happened on a Sunday, drawing moral judgements that it was the hand of God punishing the town for its ungodly ways and not observing the Sabbath. Between them, the two fires caused the destruction of approximately two hundred buildings and about £20000 worth of damage, a huge sum of money in the sixteenth century. It caused so much financial distress the Lord Treasurer agreed the town should be relieved from the taxes and subsidies it owed, and by 1601, as many as seven hundred people were on the poor-relief lists.

If Shakespeare ever visited the Chapel, he may have recognised the names of his friends and acquaintances. We will never know if this graffiti was left by William Rogers of Shrieve's House or Thomas Rogers of Harvard House, or the intentions behind it. The names may have been carved by William and Thomas's descendants or they were the names of children who never survived into adulthood. The only certainty with the 'Rogers' graffiti is that the names were carved before the last whitewashing of the Chapel as there are remnants of paint in the grooves. All three are carved at or below eye level and would have taken time to inscribe and maybe more than one visit. Whoever scratched the names into the chancel arch was evidently literate and perhaps proud of it (literacy was closely related to social status), but they also wanted these names recorded for posterity. Whatever their intention, they reach out to us from history, giving visitors today a glimpse of lives that might otherwise be forgotten.

5. 1616 onwards

THE DECADES AFTER WILLIAM SHAKESPEARE'S DEATH

The changes wrought by the Reformation were slow to take root in Stratford, but the Corporation's more obvious Protestant stance in the late-sixteenth century mirrors that of England more generally which became more firmly Protestant under Elizabeth. The Chapel was cleaned again and painted with fictive marble pillars separating recessed panels. It was now little more than a preaching venue.

Changes to graffiti after the Reformation had also been slow as the Church found it hard to eradicate deep-seated beliefs and superstitions. Nonetheless, by the end of the sixteenth century, graffiti in churches was less about spirituality and worship and more about remembrance or the marking of a visit in the way of modern graffiti. The nature of the Chapel's graffiti shifts in line with these broader trends.

House-plaques

The most obvious change after the Reformation was that graffiti was increasingly dated. This period also saw the widespread appearance of the small house-shaped 'plaques' which can be seen in churches across the country. The earliest examples of this sort of commemorative inscription date from the mid-sixteenth century but the majority are seventeenth century. They tend to include initials as well as a date. House-plaques are frequently found in small groups and get their name from the fact that they look like little houses with steeply pointed rooves, or churches. Sometimes they have crosses on top or fleurs-de-lys. There is a small house-plaque on the Chapel's chancel arch (fig. 75). If it had initials or a date within the body of the 'house', they are no longer visible. It is possible the letters carved around it might relate to it. Raking light reveals a faint criss-crossing in-fill on the roof (fig. 76).

Another memorial plaque on the chancel arch appears to be a combination of a shield and a house-plaque (fig. 77). It seems to have had both initials and a date although neither are now fully legible. The first letter of the initial appears to be an H, the second an E, with a date possibly in the 1600s. Again, it is in-filled with a criss-cross or mesh pattern.

Fig. 75. House-plaque, chancel arch, H. 6cm. *Image: Terry Galvin.*

Fig. 76. Roof detail. *Image: Rodger Palmer.*

Nearby, on the chancel arch, is another house-plaque, substantially larger than any others I have seen (fig. 78). It appears to have contained the letters H or T and E but there is no date. Remnants of paint highlight the carving. Is the same individual being memorialised here as in the shield (fig. 77)?

Fig. 77. Memorial plaque, chancel arch, north side, H. 11cm. *Image: Terry Galvin*

Fig. 78. Large house-plaque, chancel arch, north side.

It is interesting that the three examples (figs 75, 77 & 78) incorporate the criss-cross or mesh pattern. The patterns might represent bricks or roofing tiles but they might also recall the criss-cross or mesh patterns which were once thought to offer ritual protection. It is possible people continued to believe in the magic or good luck of this particular marking into the seventeenth century. There are some good examples of house-plaques elsewhere incorporating the same patterns which might indicate they had a meaning that was once universally understood, a meaning that gradually evolved and was forgotten. The meaning of graffiti can alter and is dependent upon when it was inscribed.

Despite house-plaques being so widespread, there is no consensus on what they meant or the sentiment behind them. A great deal of thought and care has gone into creating the examples in the Chapel. Each was carved at kneeling or sitting height, not dashed off arbitrarily but something someone took time and trouble over. They could be commemorating a visit - an 'I was here' proclamation - or be monuments for the dead and departed, like little gravestones carved onto the walls. This type of graffiti certainly corresponds to a time when churchyard gravestones and wall-mounted monuments began to appear. Puritan extremes which had destroyed many obvious Catholic memorials, including the churchyard cross, were halted by the Restoration of the Monarchy in 1660. This coincided with the rise of wealthier farmers, merchants and professional men who began to want a permanent memorial to themselves.

Fig. 79. Hugh Clopton's memorial plaque.

The wall-mounted monument to Hugh Clopton (died 1496), erected by his descendants and now above the priest's door in the Chapel's chancel, is dated 1708 (fig. 79). As the latest residents of New Place over the road, the Cloptons evidently wanted to draw on their association with their illustrious predecessor, perhaps seeking to reinforce their position within the town. Hugh Clopton's ambitious plans in the 1490s had brought him the perpetuity he had clearly desired when he set about rebuilding and refurbishing the Chapel, though not in the way he had envisaged.

The people who carved the graffiti plaques on the chancel arch may not have had the wealth and status of Clopton and his descendants, and religious beliefs may have changed, but the graffiti demonstrates a continuing need to leave one's mark and be remembered. The plaques can tell us about people or events that might never appear in the traditional written record. They also tell us that the Chapel was being used. Although they are typical of post-Reformation graffiti, the absence of discernible dates means they cannot be precisely dated. Again, knowing the position of the rood screen, partition wall and chambers within the chancel might help date them. Were they carved by tenants renting these chambers or were they left after the partition wall had been removed?

According to Wilfrid Puddephat, the art master at King Edward VI Grammar School in the mid-twentieth century, the wall between the nave and chancel remained until 1641 when the lower part of the rood screen was removed.[15] Puddephat suggested the wall was removed shortly after Stratford's notorious puritan vicar, the Reverend Thomas Wilson, was accused of having

'profaned the Chapple by sufferinge his children to playe at bale and other sports therein, and his servauntes to hange clothes to drye in it and his pigges and poultrie to lye and feed in it, and also his dogge to lye in it, and the pictures therein to be defaced, and the windowes broken'.

The report gives us an indication of Wilson's contempt for any outward show of reverence but also suggests some of the medieval wall-paintings may have survived until this time. Hidden behind the partition wall, were the *Legend of the Holy Cross* paintings in the chancel still visible? The interior was whitewashed throughout not long afterwards.

One of the nineteenth-century antiquarians who saw the Chapel's wall-paintings when they were first rediscovered in the early-1800s was Robert Bell Wheler. He noted that the crosses within the *Legend of the Holy Cross* paintings had been damaged by a sharp implement. Perhaps emboldened by Stratford's strengthening Puritanism whilst Thomas Wilson was vicar, those leasing the chambers may have tried to erase anything overtly religious from what were, by then, rather controversial paintings. Those sharp implements that had mutilated the wall-paintings could easily have carved the house-plaques on the

---

15 Wilfrid Puddephat discovered the *Dance of Death* painting on the north wall of the nave during the mid-twentieth-century refurbishments; he was able to reconstruct it and match the text to John Lydgate's translation of the French poem, *Danse Macabre*, from c.1430.

chancel arch. Who knows what else they might have carved on the plaster of the chancel walls? Unfortunately, the plaster was removed during the refurbishments of the early-1800s destroying both the paintings and any graffiti that was there. It is interesting that the nineteenth-century antiquarians who took so much trouble recording the paintings (and it is thanks to them that we know so much about them) do not mention any graffiti on the plasterwork, an indication perhaps that it was still so commonplace as to be unremarkable. On the other hand, it might indicate that any graffiti on the plaster had already disappeared, or even that there had been nothing there in the first place.

The leasing of chambers within the chancel might explain some of the graffiti on the chancel arch but there may be another explanation. If Puddephat was right, it was not long after the removal of the partition wall that Stratford became embroiled in the English Civil War. Like many towns, Stratford was reluctant to get involved at first but, as religious divisions hardened, the town was drawn into the horrors of *'civil butchery'* (Shakespeare, *Henry IV*, part 1, act 1, scene 1) and *'did help to wound itself'* (Shakespeare, *King John*, act 5, scene 7) in a war which Shakespeare seems to have indirectly foreseen. Without walls, open and indefensible, Stratford became a frontier zone between opposing armies relentlessly passing through. The town was occupied and re-occupied by soldiers of both sides, its residents subject to the harassment, violence and financial loss that always accompanied them. Stratford was not a garrison town, however, and it was not besieged. There were no obvious political purges and despite the inevitable disturbance, Stratford retained a measure of stability in its governance in comparison to parishes nearby.

It is often possible to detect chronological patterns in historic graffiti which is frequently left in times of war, disease or hardship. These events may be local, national or deeply personal. People have always felt the need to leave some sort of permanent memorialisation, perhaps in a place that was significant to them or had been an anchor in their lives. Leaving your mark somewhere, on the realisation that life is transient and there might not be a tomorrow, is a very human thing to do. It is not unreasonable to think that in such a deeply unsettling time, Stratford residents might have sought sanctuary in the peace and stillness of the Guild Chapel that is still so palpable today, or that passing soldiers might have been drawn to it, desperate for some solace before their next battle, instinctively carving their marks into the fine ashlar stone in a place they sensed was solid and enduring.

At first, Royalists were in ascendance in Stratford, but for most of the war, the town was nominally under Parliamentarian control. Throughout the war, troops from both sides were quartered at both the Falcon Inn, opposite the Chapel, and at New Place. New Place was still the largest and most impressive house within the borough, and still the home of Shakespeare's daughter, Susannah, and his granddaughter, Elizabeth (married to Thomas Nash). They may have hosted Charles I's queen, Henrietta, who was accompanied to Stratford by Prince Rupert in 1643.[16] Although there is no definitive evidence for Henrietta's stay at New Place, her visit features in the borough accounts which means she must have resided within the legal jurisdiction of the town, and New Place, being the largest residence available, would have been the obvious choice. Even though the Chapel was at the centre of so much upheaval, there are no reports that it suffered any damage during this time, and there is no wholesale deliberate damage discernible to the extant graffiti, perhaps because it was no longer considered obviously religious or maybe because it was no longer visible under layers of paint. Disruption to church life in Stratford as a whole was minimal, and residents experienced a degree of continuity not enjoyed in other towns where churches were routinely appropriated by troops who used them as garrisons and cookhouses or vandalised them.

The Guild Chapel's limited religious function and relatively plain appearance might be what saved it. It might also have been spared because of its proximity to Shakespeare's house and its obvious association with him. Shakespeare had enjoyed a close relationship with the inhabitants of Stratford and his reputation was growing beyond the town. His status had been recognised with his burial in Holy Trinity Church and, sometime between 1616 and 1623 (and probably before May 1619 when the puritan, Thomas Wilson, became the vicar), a bust was erected there in his memory. The *First Folio* had been published in 1623, the first collated edition of all Shakespeare's plays. Although Protestant radicals of the Civil War generation disparaged Shakespeare's work, and none of his plays was published

---

[16] Oliver Cromwell stayed overnight in Stratford at the time of the Worcester campaign in 1651, but it is not clear where he resided

during the Civil Wars, by the mid-1600s there was a growing national interest in Shakespeare's life and works, and Stratford was attracting literary pilgrims who wanted to see where he had lived. Both King Charles I and his queen, Henrietta, were Shakespeare enthusiasts and the Queen's decision to stay at New Place could have been prompted by her love of the theatre and desire to reside in the family home of the writer whose plays she had seen at court. The officers that were quartered at New Place and the Falcon Inn during the Civil War may have drawn parallels between their own situations and the characters in Shakespeare's history plays who had fought in English battles in the past. It would be understandable for them to assume Shakespeare had connections with the chapel so close to his home, especially as his plays make oblique references to living by a church. In *Much Ado About Nothing* Beatrice quips '*I can see a church by daylight*' (act 2, scene 1) while in *Twelfth Night*, Feste jokes with Viola that '*I do live by the church; for I do live at my house, and my house doth stand by the church*' (act 3, scene 1). Rather than subjecting the Chapel to the sort of unruly behaviour seen elsewhere, visiting soldiers may have treated it with a certain amount of respect, its special connection prompting, instead, a desire in them to leave their mark or remember a fellow soldier who had been lost.

6. Beyond the seventeenth century

THE RISE OF 'BARDOLOGY', TOURISM AND MODERN GRAFFITI

Puritanism was still dominant in Stratford-upon-Avon in the immediate aftermath of the Civil War, but was stopped in its tracks with the Restoration of the Monarchy in 1660 which put an end to the town's long line of puritan vicars. It is not known how long Shakespeare's granddaughter, Elizabeth, and her second husband, Sir John of Abington, continued to live next door to the Chapel but they had left New Place and moved to Abington by 1663. The house was then occupied by a variety of residents. One resident, well-known locally, was the Reverend Francis Gastrell (1701-72) who has long been vilified for cutting down the mulberry tree Shakespeare allegedly planted, and demolishing New Place, supposedly because he was fed up with tourists wanting to look at it. In reality, his destruction of New Place was more to do with his ongoing dispute with the town authorities over the level of his poor-rate contributions. In any case, Shakespeare's New Place had been pulled down in the late-seventeenth century by Sir John Clopton, a direct descendent of the original owner, Hugh Clopton. By the time Sir John acquired New Place in 1677, the house must have seemed out-of-date with its large medieval open hall, once a communal space and the focus of the house where the status of the owner could be displayed and reinforced. Now, the owner's status and that of his family and favoured guests, was marked by their segregation from servants in a society that was increasingly divided in terms of social class. Sir John built his New Place in the then fashionable Queen Anne style before gifting it to his son, Hugh, on its completion around 1702. Sir Hugh seems to have been a rather neglectful owner, on several occasions coming before the Stratford court for not maintaining his property and the area surrounding it. He is even accused of *'laying ashes and other rubbish against the Chappell wall'*. Chapel Lane at that time was in a poor state and infrequently used.

Despite a more critical attitude towards graffiti in churches by now, the remarkably well-cut names and initials of eighteenth- and nineteenth-century visitors can be seen all over our churches, cathedrals and other heritage sites.[17] Their neatness and precision suggest it was people relatively high up the social scale who left them - they were the ones with the money and freedom to make such visits. To our eyes, this graffiti might spoil historical sites but it does provide an insight into early tourism and the attitudes of those who visited. There is anecdotal evidence that early visitors to the pyramids in Egypt could even hire a man to carve inscriptions on their behalf.

In 1726, a new by-law was passed stipulating prayers were to be said in the Chapel every day except Thursday (the original market day) and it is from the early 1700s that we have the only graffito inside the Chapel that has a discernible date. Located on the south wall, to the left of the south door is the inscription 'MW 1731' (fig. 80). It has been carefully framed and deeply inscribed through the now flaking paint.

Fig. 80. MW 1731, south wall.

---

17 One of the antiquarians who documented the Chapel's wall-paintings in the early-nineteenth century was Thomas Fisher; the name Thomas Fisher has been carved onto the tomb of Richard Hill (d.1593) in Holy Trinity Church in Stratford. Was it Thomas Fisher the antiquarian who must have spent time in Stratford?

6. Beyond the seventeenth century

This inscription is almost certainly a set of dated initials, but, elsewhere, M and W are frequently found put together and many have been found amongst apotropaic graffiti, suggesting they could have a deeper significance. Even when turned upside down, MW is still MW, possibly adding to its perceived effectiveness. By the 1700s, M and VV symbols may have lost their original meaning but retained some protective function or association with good luck. Again, more research is needed but if the conjoined-V and/or M were being used as part of a set of initials, perhaps the intention was to invoke good luck upon the inscriber. The MW 1731 inscription is in the same area of the Chapel as the bulk of the IW inscriptions (fig. 14) and appears alongside several sets of the initials WE - this spot was clearly still a focus for graffiti and it would be interesting to see what lies behind the modern noticeboards fixed to the walls either side of the south door.

With the succession of smallpox outbreaks in Stratford in the first half of the eighteenth century, there was good reason for Stratfordians to want to invite good luck upon themselves. One particularly devastating outbreak of smallpox in 1736 took the lives of nearly all the schoolboys at Shakespeare's old school adjoining the Chapel; the three surviving pupils etched their initials into a beam in the upper Guildhall. The graffiti provides a moving reminder of what must have been a terrible and frightening time (fig. 81).

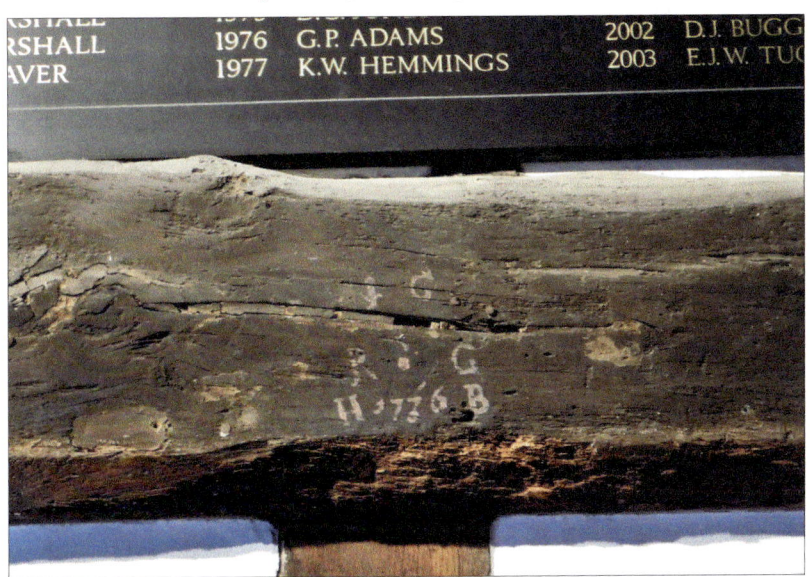

Fig. 81. Initials of the smallpox survivors in 1736, Stratford Guildhall.

Although the Chapel was now being used for daily prayers, by the late-1700s the building was deteriorating rapidly, its original shallow-pitched timber roof quite rotten. It was during the renovations and the subsequent cleaning of the Chapel in 1804-05 that some of the medieval wall-paintings were first rediscovered.[18] There was some recognition of their importance amongst the nineteenth-century antiquarians who recorded what was revealed, but the paintings in the chancel were destroyed and those exposed in the nave were quickly painted over again. The decision to cover them up almost immediately reflects a wider concern, amongst clergy in particular, of the continuing power of medieval imagery and the fear they might be a distraction from the Word of God.

As part of the refurbishments of 1804-05, the Chapel roof was replaced and outside, on the roof, alongside a plaque dedicated to the Mayor and Chamberlain of Stratford, is a lead panel containing shoe inscriptions commemorating four of the roofers (figs 82-90).

Fig. 82. Lead panel showing four shoe inscriptions.

Some of the shoe outlines have a distinctly medieval appearance, and the roofers of 1804 and 1805 may have been responding to earlier inscriptions. Records show there had been a lead panel on the roof of the Chapel dated 1625, although there is no trace of it now, and maybe the 1625 plaque was itself responding to an even earlier one.

---

18 The paintings along the north and south walls of the nave remained undisturbed owing to the retention of existing pews. These paintings were revealed during the 1950s refurbishments.

6. Beyond the seventeenth century

The lead on church rooves is frequently engraved with commemorative shoe graffiti, which would most likely have been drawn by the plumbers prior to installation.[19][20]

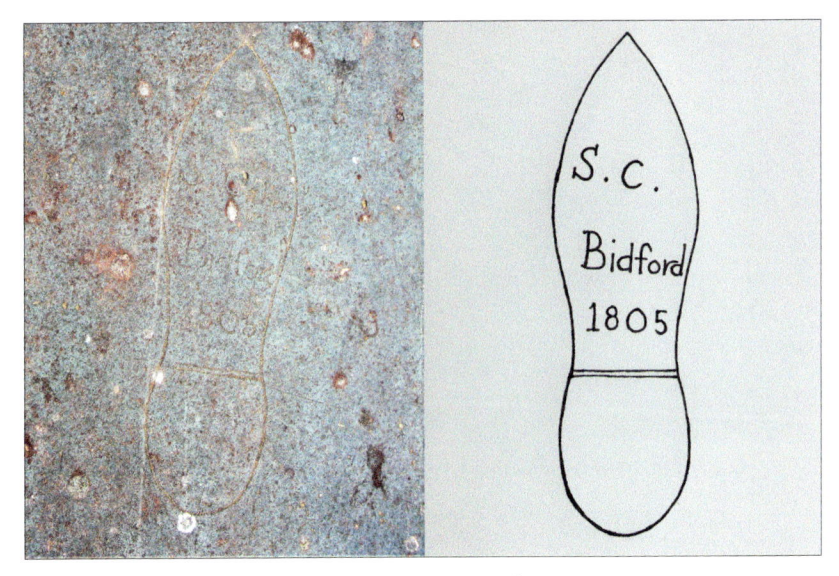

Figs 83 & 84. Top left-hand corner of the lead panel.

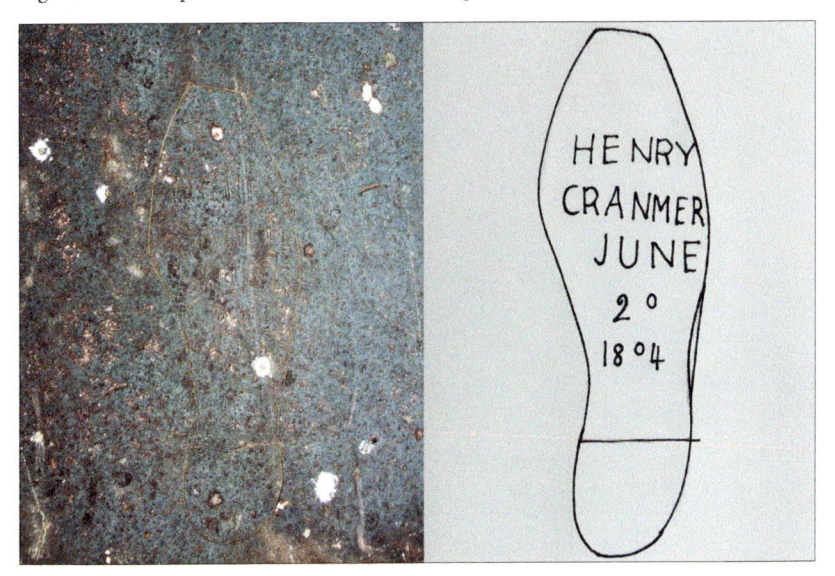

Figs 85 & 86. Bottom left-hand corner of the lead panel.

19 The Latin for lead is *plumbum*; lead was almost always used for church rooves, water pipes, baths and so on, and anyone who worked with lead was known as a 'plumber'.
20 I have been told there are over 100 shoe outlines on the lead of the roof of the Beauchamp Chapel at nearby St Mary's Church in Warwick.

85

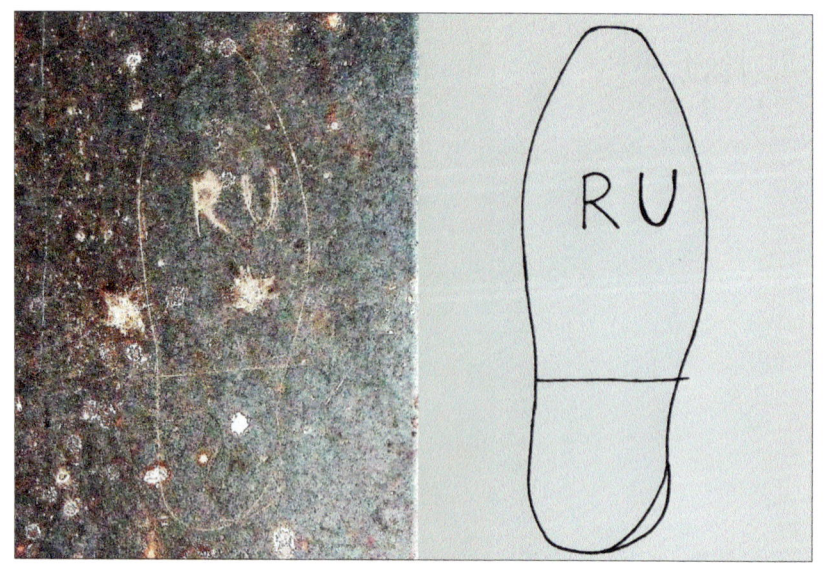

Figs 87 & 88. Top right-hand corner of the lead panel.

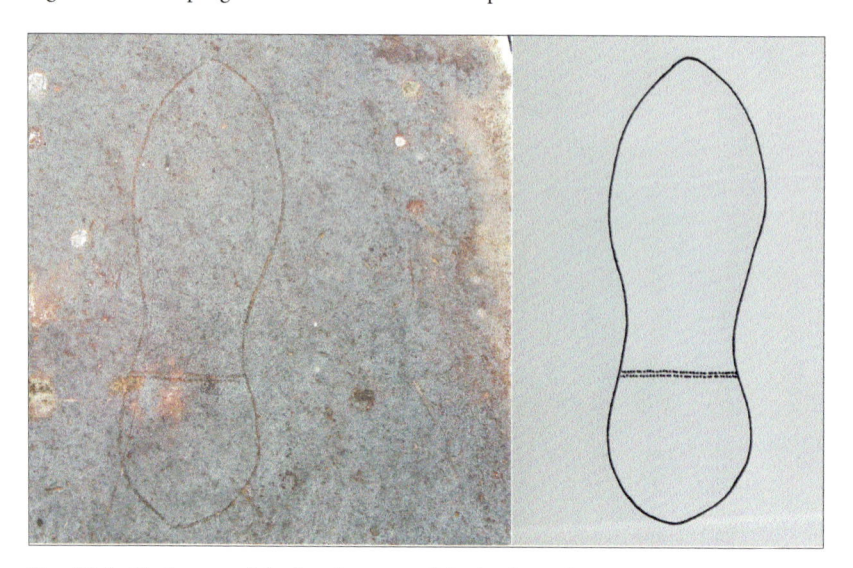

Figs 89 & 90. Bottom right-hand corner of the lead panel.

Graffiti shoes, and hands, are common inside churches too and are not necessarily left by tradesmen. Many are drawn around actual shoes and hands so are very individual and personal, and resonate with early cave art. Shoe graffiti has not always been purely memorial in nature; shoes are associated with a variety of different beliefs. One suggestion is that there is an association between medieval shoe graffiti and sites of pilgrimage. Shoes have been found hidden in voids in old buildings suggesting some sort of ritual function. The idea that shoes were apotropaic may have evolved from the story of England's unofficial saint, John Schorn, rector of North Marston (1290-1314), who reputedly cast the devil into a boot. The oldest concealed shoes date back to around the time of Shorn, but whether the tradition began with him or the legend incorporates a pre-existing practice is unclear. Shoes were not the only items to be hidden in buildings but they are the most commonly found; also hidden were clothing and other personal items as well as mummified cats and the bones of horses.[21] Nearly all of the shoes and personal items show some wear so carry the imprint of the people to whom they once belonged. They may have been hidden to protect the occupants of the house against malevolent forces, or concealed to create some kind of mutual pact between the building and its inhabitants whereby each looked after the other. The meaning may have gradually evolved so they became more of a good luck talisman. A lady's leather shoe typical of the late-eighteenth and early-nineteenth centuries was discovered in a chimney at Anne Hathaway's cottage. There are instances of shoes being hidden in buildings as late as the early-twentieth century. Even today, some people remain reluctant to remove them in case it brings bad luck.

Stratford's association with William Shakespeare was attracting ever-increasing numbers of visitors to the town, particularly after the famous actor, David Garrick, arranged a three-day Jubilee in 1769 in his honour. It was this festival which effectively triggered 'bardology' and brought the cult of Shakespeare to Stratford, establishing him as the National Poet and the Birthplace as fundamental to the celebration of his life. Even after Gastrell demolished New Place in 1759, the site drew ever greater interest, the absent presence of the house offering something different to every visitor. The site is still hugely popular and its visitors routinely cross the lane to the Chapel, to see the church that stood by Shakespeare's house.

Notwithstanding the increase in the number of people using the Chapel during the nineteenth century, there is not a great deal of graffiti that is obviously from this period. A consequence of the

---

21 Both cats and horses were attributed with the ability to see things humans cannot. During the recent refurbishment of the Falcon Inn opposite the Chapel, a significant number of foal bones were found. An explanation for their presence has not been established.

growth of Stratford's population and tourist trade was an increased congregation at Holy Trinity parish church. To accommodate worshippers in the town, a gallery was built at the west end of the Chapel in 1835 providing seating for up to three hundred people. For the first time since the Reformation, a full service was introduced in the Chapel in the morning and evening every Sunday. In his 1814 book, a *Guide to Stratford-upon-Avon*, the local antiquarian Robert Bell Wheler comments that an antechapel at the west end of the nave had been created '*by a screen which had previously separated the nave from the chancel*'. This probably refers to the medieval rood screen. It seems the panels from this screen were subsequently fitted to the west wall when the antechapel was demolished to make way for the gallery. Part of the rood screen was also used on the gallery staircase, and pieces of oak carving from the original nave roof, including the foliage bosses, were utilised in the framing of the gallery. The location of the gallery, together with the panelling and pews, meant large areas of the Chapel's walls were covered leaving little opportunity for any graffiti to be carved into the stonework. Nineteenth-century congregations may have carved graffiti onto the woodwork of the gallery but there had been a growing intolerance towards graffiti in churches since the seventeenth century, and, from the mid-nineteenth century, attitudes started to harden against all graffiti, wherever it was. By the end of the Victorian period, graffiti was widely condemned by those in authority as something undesirable: it was about this time that the word 'graffiti' was first used. Furthermore, attendance at services in the Chapel dropped at the end of the nineteenth century and continued to drop into the twentieth – with a fall in visitors there would have been a corresponding fall in graffiti.

Despite the changing attitudes of those in authority, the desire to leave one's name or record a visit, particularly in a vernacular setting, remained strong. A popular tradition amongst pilgrims to Shakespeare's Birthplace was the etching of names onto the window of the birthroom (fig. 91). Famous visitors who left their names include Sir Walter Scott, Lord Alfred Tennyson, Thomas Carlyle and the actors Helen Terry and Henry Irving. People also wrote on the walls and even on the ceilings of the birthroom, or wrote poems and dedications on pieces of paper which they then stuck to the walls. After 1860, visitors were encouraged to use visitor books instead –

although some people continued to write on the glass. The windows were preserved but the walls were painted over.

Fig. 91. Window panel from Shakespeare's birthroom.

Historic graffiti is often attributed to 'naughty schoolboys' and this is true to an extent in the Chapel (figs 92 and 93).[22] Modern graffiti scratched onto the Chapel's walls stands out brightly on the old, darkened stone and, while there is not much, what there is may well have been left by the boys of King Edward VI Grammar School as they have used the Chapel for their morning assemblies, and other events, since 1902. Graffiti was an accepted if not encouraged tradition amongst the prefects of the Grammar School until well into

---

22 There is some not-so-nice graffiti which I will not reproduce here but younger visitors to the Chapel seem drawn to it and manage to find it straight away!

the twentieth century. Boys would carve their initials into the long Jacobean table in the prefects' common room, perhaps sensing a need to leave a permanent memorial in a place they had felt secure as they faced the uncertainties of adulthood. Rather poignantly, some of the initials belong to boys who fought in the two World Wars and never came home.

Fig. 92. Dated initials, JL '75, south door surround.

Fig. 93, A tongue-in-cheek (it is to be hoped!) '666', chancel arch.

By the mid-twentieth century the Chapel had fallen into a state of disrepair – in the 1920s, there had even been talk of clearing it away on the grounds that it was *'a tumbled down old building'* and an *'obstruction to the traffic'*. In the late-1920s, after the re-discovery of the *Doom* under thick layers of whitewash, and the removal of the scripture boards that had been fitted over it, the professor of art and design at the Royal College of Art, Ernest William Tristram, recorded and conserved the *Doom*, bringing the Chapel and its paintings to the attention of the nation. Unfortunately, Tristram's use of wax dissolved in turpentine as a fixative, typical of the time, created a water-resistant surface which prevented damp from escaping, damaging the painting; in addition, the wax attracted dust and dirt and gradually the *Doom* turned brown, and it was the wax that the conservators worked so hard to remove in 2016. The Friends of the Guild Chapel was formed in 1953 with the purpose of rescuing the building. It was the Friends who oversaw the remodelling of the interior into the Oxbridge-style chapel we see today (figs 3 and 4). Records kept during the refurbishments reveal that the medieval panelling was removed from the west wall of the nave, although it is not known what happened to it afterwards. The presence of the panelling might explain why the painting, *Erthe upon Erthe*, is in such a good condition, and why the graffiti in that area has survived so well. Some of the most interesting graffiti in the Chapel is in the south-west corner. In the 1950s, when the medieval panelling was stripped out, much of the graffiti would have been obscured by layers of old paint which was only removed in 2016. It is probably just as well the graffiti has remained hidden for so long, the prevailing attitude is still that it is 'just graffiti' and it is doubtful whether there would have been much interest or appreciation of it in the 1950s. Even the medieval wall-painting *Erthe upon Erthe* was considered an 'embarrassment' architecturally speaking by Stephen Dykes Bower, the architect employed to redesign the Chapel interior, as he feared it would interfere with the new design he favoured.

The names and dates of the plumbers and electricians who have worked in the Chapel in the twentieth century can be found in the tower, the later graffiti mostly written in pencil. P. Dempsey, of Arrow Scaffolding, left his name in the lead on the roof in March 1987 in a similar way to the roofers of 1804 and 1805, scratching his name within the outline of a shoe. He finished his inscription with a very 1980s-style flourish, carving 'OK YAR!' after the date (fig. 94). I have been unable to trace P. Dempsey to remind him of his handiwork!

I recently went back up onto the roof of the Chapel to take some better photographs of the shoe inscriptions. Unfortunately, in the short space of time since 2017 when the photographs you see here were taken, the lead panel on the roof of the Guild Chapel has deteriorated to such an extent that the shoe outlines have now almost disappeared.

Fig. 94. Inscription on the lead of the roof: 'P. DEMPSEY, ARROW SCAFFOLDING, 19.3.87, OK YAR!'

Why the state of the lead should deteriorate so quickly in the last three years is a puzzle but it highlights a wider problem, and that is the urgent need for the surveying, recording and preservation of historic graffiti everywhere. Some is lost or damaged as a result of normal wear and tear. Some is being destroyed by enthusiastic visitors repeatedly touching it. The urge to run your fingers over graffiti is understandable - it is a way of engaging with the past and connecting directly with the people who carved it. However, it is the lack of awareness and understanding of the importance of graffiti as a historical resource which is causing the most damage. Graffiti is disappearing at an alarming rate as a result of careless or poor maintenance, lack of resources, and buildings being refurbished unsympathetically without a proper survey being done first. Ideally, there should be a register and official guidance on protecting graffiti. Attitudes are slowly changing, particularly at an academic level. Nevertheless, for most people, the word 'graffiti' still conjures up images of the territorial 'tags' and symbols used by street gangs, and the political slogans and street art which has proliferated since the 1960s and 70s.

This raises another question: when does modern graffiti cease to be anti-social vandalism and become valuable as a historic resource? To those who leave it, modern graffiti often has meaning and purpose and, in that sense, it is no different to the graffiti left by medieval church-goers. A new generation of street artists, such as the infamous

Banksy, have taken the idea even further, producing very personal and elaborate 'artistic' graffiti now recognised and accepted as a new art form. Meanwhile, the Chapel's historic graffiti is also inspiring new forms of creative practice and engaging new visitors to the building. Part of my work at the Chapel has involved creating graffiti trails and information sheets for the general public, along with activities for schools which meet Key Stage curriculum objectives.

Humans have always felt compelled to leave their mark, from handprints left in caves tens of thousands of years ago to the modern graffiti artists of today. There seems to be something intrinsic about the need to record one's name or make a mark in a place that is of personal significance or interest. Carving graffiti onto churches, cathedrals and other heritage sites may now be frowned upon, but people still feel the need to record their presence as the Chapel's growing visitor book affirms, and perhaps the current trend for 'selfies' is simply a modern manifestation of the need to say 'I was here'.

Bibliography

Books

Adams, Will, *A-Z of Stratford-upon-Avon. Places - People - History* (Gloucestershire: Amberley Publishing, 2018)

Alexander, Jennifer, 'Masons' Marks and the Working Practices of Medieval Stone Masons', in *Who Built Beverley Minster?*, ed. by P. S. Barnwell and A. Pacey (Reading: Spire Books, 2008)

Bearman, Robert, *The Frieze. Shakespeare's Town, Stratford-Upon-Avon: The Historic Spine*, (Stratford-upon-Avon: Stratford-upon-Avon Society, 2013)

Bearman, Robert, *Stratford-upon-Avon. A History of its Streets and Buildings* (Stratford-upon-Avon: Stratford-upon-Avon Society, 2007)

Bearman, Robert, ed., *The History of an English Borough. Stratford-upon-Avon 1196-1996* (Stroud: Sutton Publishing Limited, 1997)

Beattie, Cordelia, 'Maidens and Single Men: The Register of the Guild of the Holy Cross, Stratford-upon-Avon (1406-1535)', in *Medieval Single Women: The Politics of Social Classification in Late Medieval England* (Oxford: OUP, 2007)

Borman, Tracy, *Witches. James I and the English Witch-Hunts* (London: Vintage Books, 2014)

Bradley, Simon, *Pevsner Introductions: Churches, An Architectural Guide*, (New Haven and London: Yale University Press, 2017)

Bryson, Bill, *Shakespeare* (London: William Collins, 2016)

Champion, Matthew, *Medieval Graffiti, The Lost Voices of England's Churches* (London: Ebury, 2015)

Davies, Kathryn, *Artisan Art. Vernacular wall paintings in the Welsh Marches, 1550-1650* (Herefordshire: Logaston Press, 2008)

Davies, Owen, and Ceri Houlbrook, 'Concealed and Revealed: Magic and Mystery in the Home', *Spellbound. Magic, Ritual & Witchcraft* (Oxford: Ashmolean Museum of Art and Archaeology, 2018), pp. 67-95

Bibliography

Edmondson, Paul, Kevin Colls and William Mitchell, *Finding Shakespeare's New Place, An Archaeological Biography* (Manchester: Manchester University Press, 2016)

Fox, L., The Borough Town of Stratford-upon-Avon (Norwich: Jarrold & Sons Ltd, 1953)

Lidova, Maria, 'The Rise of the Image of Christ', *Imagining the Divine. Art and the Rise of World Religions* (Oxford: Ashmolean Museum of Art and Archaeology, 2017), pp. 51-67

MacCulloch, Diarmaid, *Reformation. Europe's House Divided, 1490-1700* (London: Penguin Books, 2004)

Macdonald, Mairi, *The Register of the Guild of the Holy Cross* (Bristol: The Dugdale Society, 2007)

Mulryne, J. R., Andrew Burnet and Margaret Shrewing, *Shakespeare's Schoolroom & Guildhall* (Peterborough: Jarrold Publishing, 2016)

Page, Sophie, 'Love in a Time of Demons: Magic and the Medieval Cosmos', *Spellbound. Magic, Ritual & Witchcraft* (Oxford: Ashmolean Museum of Art and Archaeology, 2018), pp. 19-63

Page, Sophie, *Astrology in Medieval Manuscripts* (London: The British Library, 2017)

Page, Sophie, *Magic in Medieval Manuscripts* (London: The British Library, 2017)

Parker, Keith T., *The Guild Chapel and other Guild Buildings of Stratford-upon-Avon, Based on the research of Wilfrid Puddephat* (Stratford-upon-Avon: Stratford-upon-Avon Art Society and the Guild School Association, 1987)

Pritchard, Violet, *English Medieval Graffiti* (Cambridge: Cambridge University Press, 1967)

Rosser, Gervase, *The Art of Solidarity in the Middle Ages, Guilds in England 1250-1550* (Oxford: Oxford University Press, 2017)

Scarre, Geoffrey, *Witchcraft and Magic in 16th and 17th Century Europe* (Basingstoke: Macmillan Press Ltd, 1987)

Taylor, Richard, *How to Read A Church* (London: Ebury Publishing, 2007)

Tennant, Philip, *The Civil War in Stratford-upon-Avon. Conflict and Community in South Warwickshire, 1642-1646* (Stroud: Alan Sutton Publishing Ltd, 1996)

Thomas, Keith, *Religion and the Decline of Magic* (London: Penguin, 1991)

Wheler, Robert Bell, *A Guide to Stratford-upon-Avon* (Stratford-upon-Avon: J. Ward, 1814)

Wood, Michael, *In Search of Shakespeare* (London: BBC Books, 2005)

Yorke, Trevor, *Gravestones, Tombs & Memorials* (Newbury: Countryside Books, 2014)

Journal articles

Alexander, Jennifer, 'The Introduction and Use of Masons' Marks in Romanesque Buildings in England', *Medieval Archaeology*, 51 (2007)

Bearman, Robert, 'The Early Reformation Experience in a Warwickshire Market Town: Stratford-upon-Avon, 1530-1580', *Midland History*, 32, 1 (2007)

Champion, Matthew, 'Introduction to Special Issue on New Research on Medieval and Later Graffiti', *Peregrinations: Journal of Medieval Art and Architecture*, 6, 1 (2017), pp. 1-5

Champion, Matthew, 'The Priest, the Prostitute, and the Slander on the Walls: Shifting Perceptions Towards Historic Graffiti', *Peregrinations: Journal of Medieval Art and Architecture*, 6, 1 (2017), pp. 5-37

Easton, Timothy, 'A stable door with 'protective' markings: disentangling the symbols', *Eavesdropper, the Newsletter of the Suffolk Historic Buildings Group*, 51 (2015), pp. 22-25

Easton, Timothy, 'Like the Circles That You Find…', *The Society for the Protection of Ancient Buildings* (2015), pp. 51-57

Easton, Timothy, 'Portals of Protection. Protective Symbols Found on Old Doors', *The Society for the Protection of Ancient Buildings* (2014), pp. 53-57

Easton, Timothy, 'The Use of Conjoined Vs to Protect a Dwelling', *Proc. University of Bristol Spelaeological Society*, 23, 2 (2004), pp. 127-33

Easton, Timothy and Jeremy Hodgkinson, 'Apotropaic Symbols on Cast-iron Firebacks', *Journal of the Antique Metalware Society*, 21 (2013), pp. 14-33

Fearn, Alison, 'A Light in the Darkness – the Taper Burns of Donington le Heath Manor House', *Peregrinations: Journal of Medieval Art and Architecture*, 1, 1 (2017), pp. 92-118

Fleming, Juliet, 'Wounded Walls: Graffiti, Grammatology and the Age of Shakespeare', *Criticism*, 39, 1 (1997), pp. 1-25

Giles, Kate, 'Seeing and Believing: Visuality and Space in Pre-Modern England', *World Archaeology*, 39, 1 (2007), pp. 105-21

Hamling, Tara, 'To See or Not to See? The Presence of Religious Imagery in the Protestant Household', *Art History*, 30, 2 (2007), pp. 170-97

James, Duncan, 'Carpenters' Assembly Marks in Timber-Framed Buildings', *Vernacular Architecture* (2018), 49, 1, pp. 1-31

Plesch, Veronique, 'Memory on the Wall: Graffiti on Religious Wall Paintings', *Journal of Medieval and Early Modern Studies*, 32, 1 (2002)

Revell, Louise, 'Religion and Ritual in the Western Provinces', *Greece & Rome*, Second Series, 54, 2 (2007), pp. 210-28

Williams, Becky, 'Conclusions Regarding the Study of Medieval Graffiti', *Peregrinations: Journal of Medieval Art and Architecture*, 6, 1 (2017), pp. 147-50

Williams, Becky, 'Monsters, Masons, and Markers: An overview of the graffiti at All Saints Church, Leighton Buzzard', *Peregrinations: Journal of Medieval Art and Architecture*, 6, 1 (2017), pp. 38-64

Young, Francis, 'The dissolution of the Monasteries and the Democratisation of Magic in Post-Reformation England', *Religions*, 10, 241 (2019)

Online books and articles

Cummings, Brian, 'The Reformation in Shakespeare', *Discovering Literature: Shakespeare & Renaissance* (2016) <https://www.bl.uk/shakespeare/articles/the-reformation-in-shakespeare>

Fearn, Alison and Linda Wilson, 'Which Marks?', *History Today* (2019) <https://www.historytoday.com/history-matters/which-marks>

Giles, Kate, 'Digital Creativity and the Wall Paintings of 'Shakespeare's Guildhall', Stratford-upon-Avon', *Internet Archaeology*, 44 (2017) <https://intarch.ac.uk/journal/issue44/6/toc.html>

Giles, Kate and Aleksandra McClain, 'The Devotional Image in Late Medieval England', in *The Oxford Handbook of Later Medieval Archaeology in Britain*, ed. by Christopher Gerrard and Alejandra Gutiérrez (2018) <10.1093/oxfordhb/9780198744719.013.28>

Giles, Kate, Anthony Masinton, and Geoff Arnott, 'Visualising the Guild Chapel, Stratford-upon-Avon, Digital Models as Research Tools in Buildings Archaeology', *Internet Archaeology*, 32 (2012) <https://intarch.ac.uk/journal/issue32/1/toc.html>

Hart, Cheryl, *An Analysis of the Iconographic Rosette Motif as a Means of Non-Verbal Communication: A Case Study - The Rosette Motif and its Association with Solar Symbolism (3)* (2014) https://www.academia.edu/13593099/An_Analysis_of_the_Iconographic_Rosette_Motif_as_a_Means_of_Non-Verbal_Communication_A_Case_Study_The_Rosette_Motif_and_its_Association_with_Solar_Symbolism_3_

Ireland, Rebecca, 'Saint Michael the Archangel in pre-Reformation England, and implications for the "butterfly cross" graffito', *Raking Light* (2018) <https://rakinglight.co.uk/uk/saint-michael-the-archangel-in-pre-reformation-england-and-implications-for-the-butterfly-cross-graffito/>

Kennan, Claire, 'On the threshold? The role of women in Lincolnshire's late medieval parish guilds', in *Gender in medieval places, spaces and thresholds*, ed. by Victoria Blud, Diane Heath and Einat Klafter (2019), pp. 61-74 <https://www.jstor.org/stable/j.ctv9b2tw8.11>

Macdonald, Mairi, 'Hugh Clopton', *Oxford Dictionary of National Biography* <https://doi.org/10.1093/ref:odnb/5700> [accessed 10 July 2017]

Molyneux, Nick, *Witch Markings & Magic in Old Buildings* (2016) <https://www.shakespeare.org.uk/explore-shakespeare/blogs/witch-markings-magic-old-buildings/>

Picard, Liza, 'Witchcraft, magic and religion', *Discovering Literature: Shakespeare & Renaissance* <https://www.bl.uk/shakespeare/articles/witchcraft-magic-and-religion> [accessed 26 November 2018]

Ravilious, Kate, 'Writing on the Church Wall', *Archaeology* (2015) <https://www.archaeology.org/issues/190-1509/letter-from/3554-letter-from-england-medieval-church-graffiti>

Reid, Jennifer, *Graffiti in Shakespeare's Birthroom* (2016) <https://www.shakespeare.org.uk/explore-shakespeare/blogs/graffiti-shakespeares-birthroom/>

Styles, P. ed., 'The Borough of Stratford-upon-Avon: Churches and Charities', in *A History of the county of Warwick: Volume 3, Barlichway Hundred* (2019 [1945]) <https://www.british-history.ac.uk/vch/warks/vol3/pp269-282>

Styles, P. ed., 'The Borough of Stratford-upon-Avon: Introduction and Architectural Description', in *A History of the County of Warwick: Volume 3, Barlichway Hundred* (2019 [1945]) <https://www.british-history.ac.uk/vch/warks/vol3/pp221-234>

Wheler, Robert Bell, 'History and Antiquities of Stratford-upon-Avon', in *Internet Archive* (1806) <https://archive.org/details/historyantiquiti00whel/page/n10> [accessed 28 January 2019]

Wright, James, 'Ritual protection in high-status early-modern houses', *Hidden Charms Conference*, YouTube video, added by Brian Hoggard (2016) <https://www.youtube.com/watch?v=whkbAaiz-i4>

Papers and unpublished work

Hawdon, Anthea, 'Gaming Up the Walls', paper presented on 5 October 2019 at *Making Your Mark: The First National Symposium for the Study of Historic Graffiti*, Southampton University, Southampton

Lithgow, Richard, *The Guild Chapel, Stratford-upon-Avon. Conservation of Wall Paintings. The Doom and Allegory on Mortality Treatment Record* (2017)

Page, Sophie, 'Diagrams and Magic', *Medieval Magic: Future Directions*, paper presented on the 26 June 2019 at University College London, London

Palmer, Rodger, *Renovations of the Guild Chapel, 1954-1970*, paper presented at the 17 April 2018 meeting of the Guild Chapel Volunteers, Foundation House, Stratford-upon-Avon

Parry, Glyn, *The Untold Stories of John Shakespeare*, paper presented on the 26 November 2018 at Shakespeare's Schoolroom & Guildhall, Stratford-upon-Avon

Tobit Curteis Associates LLP, *The Guild Chapel Stratford upon Avon, Condition Review and Proposal for the Conservation and Preservation of the Wall Paintings* (2016)

Websites

Apotropaios <http://www.apotropaios.co.uk/> [accessed 27 November 2019]

Norfolk Medieval Graffiti Survey <http://www.medieval-graffiti.co.uk/index.html> [accessed 23 January 2019]

Unless stated otherwise, images author's own. Back cover: Janet Hall.

Index

Astrology 26, 29-32, 42, 60
Bells 37-38, 61
Catholicism ix, 56-58, 59, 63, 76
Chancel, tenanted chambers 66-68, 77-78
Civil War 78-80, 81
Clopton, Hugh 9, 10, 12-13, 29, 51, 53, 76, 81
Consecration crosses 24-25
Dowland, Thomas 9, 10-12
Dykes Bower, Stephen 5, 91
Font 22
Friends of the Guild Chapel 2, 91
Graffiti:
   attitudes vii, ix, 16, 68, 88, 92
   broken-bar A 53-54
   burn marks 34-36
   butterfly 46-47
   chequer-board 40, 44
   compass-drawn 23-35, 40, 63
   crosses 21-23
   dating 15, 29, 36, 37, 51, 66, 68, 77
   definition vii-ix, 15-17
   house-plaques 73-77
   initials and names 15, 18-19, 48-49, 65-72, 82-83, 88-90, 91
   ladders 40
   lightning strike 36-39, 40
   location vii-viii, 16-17, 34, 43, 44
   merels 41-45, 48
   mesh/criss-cross 44-45, 73-76
   M symbol 19-20, 54
   Rogers, Thomas 70-72
   Rogers, William 68-70, 71-72
   shoes 84-87, 91-92
   Solomon's knot 26
   text inscriptions vii, 54-55
   VV/ conjoined-V 17-21, 23, 54, 63, 83

Falcon Inn 79, 80, 87
Guild of the Holy Cross vii, viii, 1, 4, 6, 7-9, 19, 22, 24, 25, 38, 39, 51, 57-58, 68, 70
Guildhall 8, 16, 17, 19, 20, 31-32, 38-39, 43, 46, 61, 64, 83
Holy Trinity Church, Stratford-upon-Avon viii, 6, 7, 12, 22, 43, 48, 53, 61, 62, 79, 82, 88
Magic 14-15, 27, 29, 42, 48, 60
Masons' marks 6-13, 36, 46, 47, 49, 50, 51, 53
New Place 6, 9, 12, 34, 38, 53, 60, 61, 62-63, 64, 76, 79-80, 81, 87
Payntor, Thomas 25
Petty school 61
Porch 2, 9, 21-22, 33-34, 47, 65
Protestantism ix, 57, 59, 60, 63, 73, 79
Puddephat, Wilfrid 77, 78
Puritanism 20, 76, 77, 79, 81
Reformation ix, 3, 7, 15, 17, 19, 20, 31, 34, 38, 44, 57-58, 59-60, 63, 68, 73, 77, 88
Rood screen 3, 17, 37, 68, 77, 88
St Mary's Church, Warwick 25, 50, 51, 85
Shakespeare, John 53, 59, 61, 71
Shakespeare, William vii, viii, ix, 6, 27, 34, 36, 38, 41, 53, 58, 59, 60-63, 64-66, 70, 71, 72, 73, 78, 79-80
Shakespeare's Birthplace 34-36, 63, 87, 88
Stratford Corporation 1, 58, 59, 61, 66, 73
Stratford Town Trust 1, 2
Virgin Mary 17-20, 25, 54
Wall-paintings 2-4, 11, 13, 17, 25, 29, 47, 54-56, 59-60, 63, 77-78, 82, 84, 90-91
Wheler, Robert Bell 77, 88
Wilson, Thomas 77, 79
Witches 14, 15, 20, 27, 35, 60

BV - #0031 - 241120 - C22 - 229/152/6 - PB - 9781913425203 - Matt Lamination